Contents

Chapter 1 *Introductory Information for Therapists*

This therapist manual is accompanied by the workbook *Reclaiming Your Life from a Traumatic Experience.* The treatment and manuals are designed for use by a therapist who is familiar with cognitive behavioral therapy (CBT) or who underwent intensive workshops for prolonged exposure by experts in this therapy. The manual will guide therapists and counselors to implement this brief CBT program that targets posttraumatic stress disorder (PTSD) following various types of trauma.

Background Information and Purpose of Emotional Processing Therapy

The overall aim of emotional processing is to help trauma survivors *emotionally process* their traumatic experiences in order to diminish PTSD and other trauma-related symptoms. The name Prolonged Exposure (PE) reflects the fact that the treatment program emerged from the long tradition of exposure therapy for anxiety disorders in which clients are helped to confront safe but anxiety-evoking situations in order to overcome their excessive fear and anxiety. At the same time, PE has emerged from the Emotional Processing Theory of PTSD, which emphasizes the central role of successfully processing the traumatic memory in the amelioration of PTSD symptoms. Throughout the book we will emphasize that emotional processing is the mechanism underlying successful reduction of PTSD symptoms.

PE includes the following procedures:

- Education about common reactions to trauma

- Breathing retraining, i.e., teaching the client how to breathe in a calming way

- Repeated in vivo exposure to situations or objects that the client is avoiding because of trauma-related distress and anxiety

- Repeated, prolonged imaginal exposure to the trauma memories (i.e., revisiting and recounting the trauma memory in imagery)

The *psychoeducation* component of PE begins in session 1 with a presentation of the overall rationale for the treatment to the client. In addition to providing an overview of the program, we introduce the idea that avoidance of trauma reminders serves to maintain PTSD symptoms and trauma-related distress and that PE directly counteracts such avoidance. This rationale is repeated and elaborated in the next several sessions with the introduction of the core interventions of PE: imaginal and in vivo exposure. Psychoeducation continues in session 2 with a discussion of Common Reactions to Trauma, in which the therapist reviews with the client common symptoms, emotions, and behaviors that occur in the wake of traumatic experiences, with the aim of eliciting and discussing the client's own reactions to the traumatic experiences and normalizing these reactions in the context of PTSD.

Breathing retraining is introduced in session 1 with the aim of providing the client with a useful and handy skill to reduce general tension and anxiety that interfere with daily functioning (e.g., at work). In our experience, some clients find this technique extremely useful and use it often, while others do not. With a few exceptions, we instruct the clients not to use breathing retraining during exposure exercises because we want them to experience their ability to cope with trauma-related memories and situations without special devices. In our view, the breathing skill is not critical to the process and outcome of PE.

In vivo exposure to safe situations, activities, places, and objects that the client is avoiding because of trauma-related anxiety and distress is introduced in session 2. In each session thereafter, the therapist and client choose which exercises the client should practice, taking into consideration the client's level of distress and ability to complete the assignments successfully. For the most part, the client conducts the in vivo exercises as homework between sessions, but if an exercise is particularly difficult, the therapist and the client may do it together.

Imaginal exposure, revisiting the trauma memory in imagery, is initiated in session 3. It consists of the client visualizing and recounting the traumatic event aloud and is conducted in each treatment session from then on. The narrative is audiotaped, and the client is instructed to listen to the recording from that week's session for homework. As noted above, these two interventions—imaginal and in vivo exposure—comprise the core procedures of PE.

The aim of in vivo and imaginal exposure, as explained to clients in the overall rationale for treatment, is to enhance emotional processing of traumatic events by helping them face the trauma memories and the situations that are associated with them. In doing so, the clients learn that the memories of the trauma, and the situations or activities that are associated with these memories, are not the same as the trauma itself. They learn that they can safely experience these trauma reminders, that the anxiety and distress that initially result from confrontations with these reminders decrease over time, and that they can tolerate this distress. Ultimately, the treatment helps PTSD sufferers reclaim their lives from the fear and avoidance that restrict their existence and render them dysfunctional.

Diagnostic Criteria for Posttraumatic Stress Disorder

Posttraumatic stress disorder (PTSD) is included in the current *Diagnostic and Statistical Manual of Mental Disorders, 4th Edition, Text Revision* (*DSM-IV-TR*; APA, 2000) as an anxiety disorder that may develop in the wake of an event that is experienced or witnessed and involves actual or perceived threat to life or physical integrity. Furthermore, the person's emotional reaction to this event is characterized by horror, terror, or helplessness. Three clusters of symptoms characterize PTSD: reexperiencing, avoidance, and hyperarousal.

DSM-IV-TR Criteria for Posttraumatic Stress Disorder

A. The person has been exposed to a traumatic event in which both of the following were present:
   1. The person experienced, witnessed, or was confronted with an event or events that involved actual or threatened death or

serious injury, or a threat to the physical integrity of self or others.

    2. The person's response involved intense fear, helplessness, or horror.

B. The traumatic event is persistently reexperienced in one (or more) of the following ways:

    1. Recurrent and intrusive distressing recollections of the event, including images, thoughts, or perceptions

    2. Recurrent distressing dreams of the event

    3. Acting or feeling as if the traumatic event were recurring (includes a sense of reliving the experience, illusions, hallucinations, and dissociative flashback episodes, including those that occur on awakening or when intoxicated)

    4. Intense psychological distress at exposure to internal or external cues that symbolize or resemble an aspect of the traumatic event

    5. Physiological reactivity on exposure to internal or external cues that symbolize or resemble an aspect of the traumatic event

C. Persistent avoidance of stimuli associated with the trauma and numbing of general responsiveness (not present before the trauma), as indicated by three or more of the following:

    1. Efforts to avoid thoughts, feelings, or conversations associated with the trauma

    2. Efforts to avoid activities, places, or people that arouse recollections of the trauma

    3. Inability to recall an important aspect of the trauma

    4. Markedly diminished interest or participation in significant activities

    5. Feeling of detachment or estrangement from others

    6. Restricted range of affect (e.g., unable to have loving feelings)

    7. Sense of foreshortened future (e.g., does not expect to have a career, marriage, children, or a normal life span)

D. Persistent symptoms of increased arousal (not present before the trauma), as indicated by two or more of the following:

    1. Difficulty falling or staying asleep

2. Irritability or outbursts of anger
3. Difficulty concentrating
4. Hypervigilance
5. Exaggerated startle response

E. Duration of the disturbance (symptoms in Criteria B, C, and D) is more than 1 month.

F. The disturbance causes clinically significant distress or impairment in social, occupational, or other important areas of functioning.
   Specify if:
   Acute: Duration of symptoms is less than 3 months
   Chronic: Duration of symptoms is 3 months or more
   Specify if:
   With Delayed Onset: Onset of symptoms occurs at least 6 months after the stressor

The symptoms of PTSD are quite common immediately after traumatic events, but for most trauma survivors, through natural recovery, the intensity and frequency of these symptoms decrease over time. However, for the minority, the PTSD symptoms persist, become chronic, and interfere with daily functioning. According to the *DSM-IV-TR*, the diagnosis of acute PTSD is made when symptoms persist for more than 1 month following the trauma and cause clinically significant distress or impairment. PTSD becomes chronic when the symptoms persist for 3 months or more and is considered as delayed onset when symptoms do not manifest until at least 6 months posttrauma.

Prevalence

Traumatic events occur quite frequently, with up to 60% of the U.S. population exposed to at least one traumatic event in their lifetime (Kessler, Sonnega, Bromet, Hughes, & Nelson, 1995). In testament to the powers of recovery, lifetime rates of PTSD in the general U.S. population range from approximately 8%–14% (Breslau, 1998; Breslau, Davis, Andreski, & Peterson, 1991; Kessler et al., 1995), indicating that most trauma survivors have never experienced PTSD.

Studies have consistently shown that women are twice as likely to develop PTSD as are men (e.g., Kessler et al., 1995); possible reasons for this phenomenon are discussed by Tolin and Foa (2006). Studies indicate that most of the recovery occurs within the first 3 months (e.g., Rothbaum, Foa, Riggs, Murdock, & Walsh, 1992) and that when PTSD persists a year after the traumatic event it is unlikely to remit without treatment (Kessler et al., 1995). PTSD is often associated with high rates of comorbidity of other disorders, particularly mood disorders, other anxiety disorders, and substance abuse disorders (Kessler et al., 1995). Moreover, health problems are more prevalent in trauma survivors with PTSD than in those without PTSD (Schnurr & Green, 2004). PTSD is also associated with poor quality of life and with great economic cost (e.g., loss of work days). Thus, PTSD not only causes psychological distress to the sufferers but also has grave public health and economic implications.

Development of This Treatment Program and Evidence Base

To date, variants of exposure therapy including Prolonged Exposure (PE) have received the most empirical evidence for their efficacy in treating PTSD. The strong efficacy of exposure therapy with or without other cognitive behavioral components has been demonstrated in a wide range of populations, including female sexual assault survivors, survivors of childhood abuse, and mixed gender samples exposed to a variety of traumatic experiences, such as traffic accidents, torture, criminal victimization, and combat (see Cahill, Hembree, & Foa, 2006). In our work at the Center for the Treatment and Study of Anxiety (CTSA) at the University of Pennsylvania, we have developed PE for the last 20 years through well-controlled studies in which we provided this treatment to hundreds of clients. In addition, we have trained numerous therapists in a variety of settings and countries to implement the treatment. Our clinical experiences and the results of our studies over these years have guided the evolution of PE to its current form, which is detailed in the chapters that follow. In addition, our experience as trainers has attuned us to the questions and concerns therapists have regarding the effective implementation of PE.

The conception of PE began with the introduction of PTSD into the *DSM-III* as an anxiety disorder in 1980. Since PTSD did not formally exist prior to this time, we had no empirical knowledge of how to best treat the disorder. Nevertheless, in 1980 we already had substantial empirical knowledge that variants of exposure therapy were effective in ameliorating symptoms of anxiety disorders such as specific phobias, panic disorder, and obsessive-compulsive disorder. In addition, those of us who worked in anxiety disorder clinics treated patients whose anxiety symptoms emanated from traumatic experiences; exposure therapy reduced those symptoms, although it was not called "PTSD" then.

The placement of PTSD among the anxiety disorders, together with studies demonstrating that certain exposure programs were more effective for one anxiety disorder than for another (e.g., systematic desensitization was more effective for specific phobias than for agoraphobia), provided the impetus to develop an exposure therapy program that was tailored to the specific phenomenology of PTSD. With these considerations in mind, in 1982 we applied for a National Institute of Mental Health grant to develop Prolonged Exposure therapy for trauma survivors who suffered from chronic PTSD and to study its efficacy with rape survivors. The first study began in 1984. Since then, with continuous funding from the National Institute of Mental Health (NIMH) and more recently from the National Institute on Alcohol Abuse and Alcoholism (NIAAA), we have been studying PE with different client populations, with the aim of elucidating both the outcome and the process of this treatment program.

As noted above, over the past two decades we have conducted a series of treatment outcome studies designed to test the efficacy and effectiveness of PE and to compare it with other forms of cognitive behavioral therapy. All of these studies utilized a randomized controlled design using the gold standard methodology for studies examining the efficacy of psychosocial treatments (Foa & Meadows, 1997). These included the use of treatment manuals, specified inclusion and exclusion criteria, independent blind assessment of outcome, assessment of change via standardized validated measures, and treatment fidelity monitoring.

In the first study (Foa, Rothbaum, Riggs, & Murdock, 1991), 45 female rape victims with chronic PTSD were treated with nine sessions of PE, stress inoculation training (SIT), or supportive counseling (SC), and their benefit from treatment was compared with that of clients who were told that their treatment would be delayed (wait list control). Treatment sessions were 90 minutes long and were conducted twice weekly. Therapists were master's- or PhD-level psychologists. At the end of treatment, those receiving PE and SIT, and to a lesser extent those receiving supportive counseling, significantly improved from pre- to posttreatment, while those on the wait list did not. At a 1-year follow-up, those who received PE continued to improve, while the other groups maintained their gains. These results, although based on a small number of women, were promising.

In a second study (Foa, Dancu, et al., 1999), 97 female survivors of rape and nonsexual assault with chronic PTSD were treated with nine twice-weekly 90-minute sessions of PE, SIT, or a combination of the two, and their outcome was again compared with that of clients whose treatment was delayed. Clients who were treated with PE alone, SIT alone, or the combination of PE and SIT showed substantial reduction in PTSD severity and depression, whereas those on the wait list showed no improvement. In fact, immediately after treatment ended, only 35% of the women receiving PE, 42% of those receiving SIT, and 46% of those receiving PE/SIT retained a diagnosis of PTSD. Contrary to our expectation that the PE/SIT group would benefit most from their treatment, PE alone was superior to SIT and PE/SIT on several indices of benefit from treatment. Specifically, the effect sizes (a measure of the degree of treatment benefit) were considerably larger for PE alone than for SIT and PE/SIT, as was the number of clients who improved on all primary measures: PTSD, general anxiety, and depression. Similar results were obtained at a 1-year follow-up. The failure of the combination of PE and SIT to provide more benefit than PE alone was puzzling. One explanation was that SIT included several techniques and, in combination with PE, might have overloaded the client.

This explanation led us to conduct a third study (Foa, Hembree, et al., 2005) in which we compared PE alone with PE combined with only one additional technique, cognitive restructuring (CR), which has been found beneficial for other anxiety disorders such as panic disorder. The augmentation effect of CR when added to PE was examined in 179 women with chronic PTSD resulting from rape, nonsexual assault, and/or childhood sexual abuse. Of these, 74 women were treated by MA-level clinicians with degrees in counseling or social work in a community-based rape treatment center in Philadelphia called Women Organized Against Rape (WOAR). Prior to the WOAR therapists' involvement in the study, they had worked with sexual assault survivors but did not have training or experience with CBT. Standard clinical practice at WOAR at that time consisted of crisis intervention and individual and group supportive counseling. The study participants at WOAR were women who presented for sexual assault–related services at WOAR because of the clinic's reputation in the city.

The remaining 105 women who participated in this study were treated by clinicians from the CTSA, an academic research clinic specializing in the study and treatment of anxiety disorders; the clinicians were PhD-level clinical psychologists with extensive experience in CBT, and especially PE. All study therapists (both at WOAR and CTSA) received initial, intensive training in PE and in trauma-focused cognitive restructuring by experts (Edna Foa, PhD, and Constance V. Dancu, PhD, for PE and David M. Clark, PhD, of Oxford University, for CR).

The initial 5-day PE workshop included an overview of the theory and efficacy data supporting the use of PE as well as instruction in how to implement PE. Much of the time was devoted to practicing how to deliver the overall rationale for the treatment and the rationales for imaginal and in vivo exposure, and how to implement these exposure techniques. A second 5-day workshop was devoted to cognitive restructuring. This training in how to implement CR was tailored to trauma survivors and focused on the impact trauma has on the survivor's thoughts and beliefs about the self, others, and the world.

The women who participated in the study received between 9 and 12 90-minute sessions of therapy, delivered once per week. The results of this study indicated that both PE and PE/CR resulted in greater reductions in symptoms of PTSD, anxiety, and depression than those on the wait list both at posttreatment and at a 1-year follow-up. The two treatments were equally effective, although effect sizes were again larger in PE alone than in PE combined with CR.

Several other researchers have used PE in comparative treatment studies and found it similarly effective. For example, Resick et al. (2002) compared PE alone with cognitive processing therapy (CPT), a form of cognitive therapy for rape survivors that includes some exposure in the form of writing and repeatedly reading the trauma narrative, in women with rape-related PTSD. In comparison to the wait list, both PE and CPT yielded significant improvement in PTSD symptoms and depression, and the gains were maintained through the 9-month follow-up period. There were no significant differences between groups on these measures, but CPT appeared to have a slight advantage over PE on two secondary measures of guilt.

Rothbaum et al. (2005), in a study of women with sexual assault–related PTSD, compared PE with eye movement desensitization and reprocessing (EMDR; Shapiro, 1989, 1995) and with wait-list control. In EMDR, another therapeutic approach that has been used for treatment of trauma-related problems, the therapist asks the client to generate images, thoughts, and feelings about the trauma, to evaluate their aversive qualities, and to make alternative cognitive appraisals of the trauma or their behavior during it. During these various stages, the therapist elicits rapid saccadic eye movements. Results indicated that, compared with the wait list, both treatments produced significant improvement in PTSD, depression, and anxiety, and the two active treatments did not differ at the posttreatment assessment. However, the PE group was superior to the EMDR group on a composite measure of functioning taken at a follow-up assessment 6 months after the end of treatment.

Other researchers in the United States and abroad have used imaginal and in vivo exposure with and without other CBT components in numerous studies. Taken together, the results of these studies generally indicate that exposure treatments like PE are highly effective at ameliorating the symptoms of PTSD, depression, and anxiety, and in comparison with other forms of CBT they achieve comparable outcomes. Moreover, several studies in addition to that of Foa et al. (2005) have found that adding various CBT techniques to PE did not enhance the benefit of PE alone (for a review see Foa, Rothbaum, & Furr, 2003). Therefore, we have abandoned the inclusion of other formal CBT techniques with PE.

Can community clinicians deliver PE effectively? The Foa et al. (2005) study described above was designed not only to examine the augmenting effects of CR, but also to answer this important question by comparing the treatment outcome of clients who received their treatment from WOAR MA-level counselors with those who received their treatment from CTSA PhD-level clinicians. The results indicated no differences in treatment outcome between the two groups of clients. This was the first study to show that PE can be successfully transported to a community setting and implemented effectively by non-CBT experts, with the clients self-referred to WOAR. We are currently conducting additional dissemination studies to determine how well the community therapists continue to use PE after expert supervision is withdrawn and how PE compares to "treatment as usual" in community settings.

The dissemination of PE to WOAR counselors was simplified by the fact that both CTSA and WOAR are located in the same city, Philadelphia. In order to extend the dissemination of PE beyond Philadelphia, we have developed a second model of treatment dissemination aimed at reducing experts' involvement in the dissemination process, thus not only limiting costs but also enabling dissemination to places that do not have access to local experts. In this model, community clinicians come to train in our clinic for various lengths of time with the expectation that they will go back to their communities, where they will train and supervise local clinicians in the delivery of PE.

While we have been conducting PE workshops around the world, the most systematic dissemination program was instituted in Israel during the past 4 years, where Foa and her colleagues delivered many PE workshops. Consistent with the model described above, clinicians working in treatment centers for recent victims of terrorist attacks and/or patients with combat-related chronic PTSD have received training to become supervisors at our center, lasting from 2 to 5 weeks. Organizations (e.g., hospitals, universities, the Joint Distribution Committee) and government institutions (e.g., the Israeli Defense Force) then sponsored 5-day workshops for clinicians whose work focuses on trauma-related psychological disturbance, with an emphasis on PTSD.

The program to disseminate PE was built in part on our accumulation of experiences described earlier (e.g., training therapists for studies with WOAR). After the workshops, several supervision groups were formed. Supervisors were clinicians who were trained especially for this role in our center. The supervision groups meet regularly, viewing tapes and discussing the clients' treatment plans and progress. Although we remain available for consultation to the supervisors on an as-needed basis, our involvement as consultants has been very limited.

Results from clients treated in the supervision groups have been very impressive. For example, in Tel Hashomer Hospital, the first 10 clients who received PE were all men. Most had chronic PTSD related to combat; some had suffered from PTSD symptoms for 30 years and had been in psychiatric treatment for many years with little or no improvement. After 10–15 sessions of PE, the mean reduction of symptoms was 58%. This outcome was quite impressive and is comparable to results at our clinic and at WOAR with women victims of sexual and nonsexual assault. A randomized, controlled study that compared PE with treatment as usual demonstrated results similar to those in the open studies (Nacasch et al., 2003).

As a result of the large body of research supporting the effectiveness of PE, the treatment program was awarded a 2001 Exemplary Substance Abuse Prevention Program Award by the U.S. Department of Health and Human Services, Substance Abuse and Mental Health Services Administration (SAMHSA), and was designated as a Model Program for national dissemination.

PE Model of PTSD: Emotional Processing Theory

As mentioned earlier, the conceptual backbone of Prolonged Exposure is Emotional Processing Theory, which was developed by Foa and Kozak (1985, 1986) as a framework for understanding the anxiety disorders and the mechanisms underlying exposure therapy. The starting point of Emotional Processing Theory is the notion that fear is represented in memory as a cognitive structure that is a "program" for escaping danger. The fear structure includes representations of the feared stimuli (e.g., bear), the fear responses (e.g., heart rate acceleration), and the meaning associated with the stimuli (e.g., bears are dangerous) and responses (e.g., fast heartbeat means I am afraid). When a fear structure represents a realistic threat, we refer to it as a normal fear structure that acts as a template for effective action to threat. Thus, feeling fear or terror in the presence of a bear and acting to escape are appropriate responses and can be seen as normal and adaptive fear reactions.

According to Foa and Kozak (1986), a fear structure becomes pathological when (1) associations among stimulus elements do not accurately represent the world, (2) physiological and escape/avoidance responses are evoked by harmless stimuli, (3) excessive and easily triggered response elements interfere with adaptive behavior, and (4) harmless stimulus and response elements are erroneously associated with threat meaning. Foa and Kozak (1985) suggested that the anxiety disorders reflect specific pathological structures and that treatment reduces anxiety disorder symptoms via modifying the pathological elements in the fear structure. These modifications are the essence of emotional processing, which is the mechanism underlying successful treatment, including exposure therapy. According to Foa and Kozak, two conditions are necessary for successful modification of a pathological fear structure, and thereby amelioration of the anxiety symptoms. First, the fear structure must be activated, otherwise it is not available for modifications; second, new information that is incompatible with the erroneous information embedded in the fear structure must be available and incorporated into the fear structure. When this occurs, information that used to evoke anxiety symptoms no longer does so.

Deliberate, systematic confrontation with stimuli (e.g., situations, objects) that are feared despite being safe or having low probability of producing harm meets these two conditions. How so? Exposure to feared stimuli results in the activation of the relevant fear structure and at the same time provides realistic information about the likelihood and the cost of feared consequences. In addition to the fear of external threat (e.g., being attacked again), the person may have erroneous cognitions about anxiety itself that are disconfirmed during exposure, such as the belief that anxiety will never end until the situation is escaped or that the anxiety will cause the person to "lose control" or "go crazy." This new information is encoded during the exposure therapy session, altering the fear structure and mediating between-session habituation upon subsequent exposure to the same or similar stimuli, thereby resulting in symptom reduction.

Foa and colleagues subsequently refined and elaborated on the original theory of emotional processing, offering a comprehensive theory of PTSD that accounts for natural recovery from traumatic events, the development of PTSD, and the efficacy of cognitive behavioral therapy in the treatment and prevention of chronic PTSD (Foa, Steketee, & Rothbaum,

1989; Foa & Riggs, 1993; Foa & Jaycox, 1999; Foa & Cahill, 2001; Foa, Huppert, & Cahill, 2006).

According to Emotional Processing Theory, the fear structure underlying PTSD is characterized by a particularly large number of stimulus elements that are erroneously associated with the meaning of danger, as well as representations of physiological arousal and of behavioral reactions that are reflected in the symptoms of PTSD. Because of the large number of stimuli that are perceived as dangerous, individuals with PTSD perceive the world as entirely dangerous. In addition, representations of how the person behaved during the trauma, their subsequent symptoms, and negative interpretation of the PTSD symptoms are associated with the meaning of self-incompetence. These two broad sets of negative cognitions ("The world is entirely dangerous," "I am completely incompetent to cope with it") further promote the severity of PTSD symptoms, which in turn reinforce the erroneous cognitions (for more details, see Foa & Rothbaum, 1998).

Trauma survivors' narratives of their trauma have been characterized as being fragmented and disorganized (e.g., Kilpatrick, Resnick, & Freedy, 1992). Foa and Riggs (1993) proposed that the disorganization of trauma memories is the result of several mechanisms known to interfere with processing of information that is encoded under conditions of intense distress. Consistent with hypotheses that PTSD would be associated with a disorganized memory for the trauma, Amir, Stafford, Freshman, and Foa (1998) found that a lower level of articulation of the trauma memory shortly after an assault was associated with higher PTSD symptom severity 12 weeks later. In a complementary finding, Foa, Molnar, and Cashman (1995) reported that treatment of PTSD with prolonged exposure was associated with increased organization of the trauma narrative. Moreover, reduced fragmentation was associated with reduced anxiety, and increased organization was associated with reduced depression.

Natural Recovery or Development of Chronic PTSD

As noted earlier, high levels of PTSD symptoms are common immediately following a traumatic event, and then most individuals will show a decline in their symptoms over time. However, a significant minority of trauma survivors fails to recover and continues to suffer from PTSD symptoms for years. Foa and Cahill (2001) proposed that natural recovery results from emotional processing that occurs in the course of daily life. This process occurs through repeated activation of the trauma memory, engagement with trauma-related thoughts and feelings and sharing them with others, and being confronted with situations that serve as reminders of the trauma. In the absence of additional traumas, these natural exposures contain information that disconfirms the common posttrauma perception that the world is a dangerous place and that the person is incompetent. In addition, talking about the event with supportive others and thinking about it help the survivor organize the memory in a meaningful way.

Why, then, do some trauma victims go on to develop chronic PTSD? Within the framework of Emotional Processing Theory, the development of chronic PTSD is conceptualized as a failure to adequately process the traumatic memory because of extensive avoidance of trauma reminders. Accordingly, therapy for PTSD should promote emotional processing. Paralleling natural recovery, PE for the treatment of PTSD is assumed to work through activation of the fear structure, by the clients deliberately confronting trauma-related thoughts, images, and situations via imaginal and in vivo exposure, and learning that their perceptions about themselves and the world are inaccurate.

How does PE lead to improvement in PTSD symptoms? Avoidance of trauma memories and related reminders is maintained through the process of negative reinforcement; that is, through the reduction of anxiety in the short run. In the long run, however, avoidance maintains trauma-related fear by impeding emotional processing. By confronting trauma memories and reminders, PE blocks negative reinforcement of cognitive and behavioral avoidance, thereby reducing one of the primary factors that maintain PTSD. Another mechanism involved in emotional processing is habituation of anxiety, which disconfirms erroneous beliefs that anxiety will last forever or will diminish only upon escape. Clients also learn that they can tolerate their symptoms and that having them does not result in "going crazy" or "losing control," fears commonly held by individuals with PTSD.

Imaginal and in vivo exposure also help clients to differentiate the traumatic event from other similar but nondangerous events. This allows them to see the trauma as a specific event occurring in space and time, which helps to refute their perception that the world is entirely dangerous and that they are completely incompetent. Importantly, PTSD clients often report that thinking about the traumatic event feels to them as if it is "happening right now." Repeated imaginal exposure to the trauma memory promotes discrimination between the past and present by helping clients realize that, although remembering the trauma can be emotionally upsetting, they are not in the trauma again and therefore thinking about the event is not dangerous. Repeatedly revisiting and recounting the trauma memory also provides the client with the opportunity to accurately evaluate aspects of the event that are actually contrary to their beliefs about danger and self-incompetence that may otherwise be overshadowed by the more salient threat-related elements of the memory. For example, individuals who feel guilty about not having done more to resist an assailant may come to the realization that the assault likely would have been more severe had they resisted. All of these changes reduce PTSD symptoms and bring about a sense of mastery and competence. The corrective information that is provided via imaginal and in vivo exposure is further elaborated during the processing part of the session that follows the imaginal exposure.

Risks and Benefits of This Treatment Program

Benefit

Twenty years of research on PE, some of it described in this chapter, have yielded findings that clearly support the excellent efficacy of PE as a treatment for PTSD. Nearly all studies have found that PE reduces not only PTSD but also other trauma-related problems, including depression, general anxiety, anger, and guilt. It helps people to reclaim their lives.

Risks

The primary risks associated with PE therapy are discomfort and emotional distress when confronting anxiety-provoking images, memories, and situations in the course of treatment. The procedures of PE are intended to promote engagement with the range of emotions associated with the traumatic memory (e.g., anxiety, fear, sadness, anger, shame, guilt) in order to help the client process the traumatic memories. As will be described in detail in chapter 8, during PE the therapist not only should be supportive and empathic in guiding the client through the processing of the trauma memory but should also monitor the client's distress and intervene when necessary to modulate the level of emotional engagement and associated discomfort. When recommending PE to a trauma survivor, the therapist should explain that disclosing trauma-related information and working to emotionally process these painful experiences in therapy often cause temporary increased emotional distress and can also lead to a temporary exacerbation of psychiatric symptoms, including PTSD, anxiety, and depression. This is described to clients as "feeling worse before you feel better." However, in a sample of 75 women receiving PE for assault-related PTSD, this temporary exacerbation of symptoms was not associated with worse outcome or with premature termination of treatment (Foa, Zoellner, Feeny, Hembree, & Alvarez-Conrad, 2002). Moreover, while some clients fail to benefit from this therapy, there are only a handful of case reports of symptoms worsening after exposure therapy.

Alternative Treatments

Although an extensive review of studies investigating cognitive behavioral treatments for PTSD is beyond the scope of this therapist manual, our own research findings are neither unique nor isolated. In general, many studies over the past 20 years have found exposure therapy effective in reducing PTSD and other trauma-related pathology, rendering it the most empirically validated approach among the psychosocial treatments for PTSD and one designated by expert consensus as a first-line intervention (Foa, Davidson, & Frances, 1999). In addition to PE and other variants of exposure therapy, the CBT programs that have been empirically examined and found effective include stress inoculation training (SIT), cognitive processing therapy (CPT), cognitive therapy (CT), and eye movement desensitization and reprocessing (EMDR). For detailed reviews, see Foa & Meadows, 1997; Rothbaum, Meadows, Resick, & Foy, 2000; Harvey, Bryant, & Tarrier, 2003; and Cahill & Foa, 2004.

Experts consider the selective serotonergic reuptake inhibitors (SSRIs) to be the first-line pharmacological treatment for PTSD (Foa, Davidson, et al., 1999; Friedman, Davidson, Mellman, & Southwick, 2000). Moreover, to date, the only medications to receive indications for treatment of PTSD from the U.S. Food and Drug Administration are two SSRIs: sertraline (Zoloft) and paroxetine (Paxil). A number of randomized controlled trials have found SSRIs to be superior to placebo, and most studies of SSRIs have generally found a significant reduction in all symptom clusters of PTSD: reexperiencing, avoidance, and arousal. They are also considered useful agents because of their efficacy in improving comorbid disorders such as depression, panic disorder, and obsessive-compulsive disorder and because of their relatively low side-effect profile.

More research needs to be conducted to expand our knowledge of pharmacological treatments for PTSD. Research is also needed to compare the relative efficacy of medications, psychosocial therapies, and their combination. Although many PTSD sufferers receive such combined treatment, little is known about its efficacy or about specific treatment combinations. We recently completed a study designed to determine whether augmenting sertraline with PE would result in greater improvement than continuation with sertraline alone. Outpatient men and women with chronic PTSD completed 10 weeks of open label sertraline and then were randomly assigned to 5 additional weeks of sertraline alone ($n = 31$) or sertraline plus 10 sessions of twice-weekly PE ($n = 34$). Results indicated that sertraline led to a significant reduction in PTSD severity after 10 weeks but was associated with no further reductions after 5 more weeks. Participants who received PE showed further reduction in PTSD severity. This augmentation effect was observed only for participants who showed a partial response to medication. Thus, the addition of PE to sertraline for PTSD improved the outcome for individuals experiencing a less than full response to the medication (Rothbaum et al., 2006).

In addition, in our studies and in our nonstudy clinical practice, it is common for clients to enter PE treatment already taking an SSRI or other appropriate medication for their PTSD and/or depression. For study measurement purposes, we merely require that the person be on a stable dose of the medication for at least 3 months prior to commencing treatment. On the basis of our experiences, we have no reason to think that concurrent medication treatment hinders the process or outcome of therapy with PE. Indeed, especially for PTSD clients presenting with severe, comorbid depression, ongoing pharmacotherapy may be quite helpful and allow them to participate fully in the PE treatment.

Outline of This Treatment Program

The treatment program consists of 10–15 weekly or twice-weekly treatment sessions that are generally 90 minutes each. This manual is divided into chapters that provide instructions about how to conduct each session and how to present the material to the client.

Each session includes an outline of what is to be accomplished (with suggested time frames), the information that you will convey to your client, the techniques you will use and how to use them, and what homework to assign to your client. The client will receive a workbook that contains all necessary handouts and homework forms. Each session should be audiotaped for the client to review as part of the homework each week. In addition, a separate audiotape will be made during the breathing retraining in session 1 for the client to use at home to practice the breathing skill. We record the breathing practice on a tape for several minutes and give it to the client for practice at home. Finally, beginning in session 3, two audiotapes will be used in each session, as the imaginal exposure (revisiting and recounting the traumatic memory) will be recorded alone on one tape in order to facilitate the homework of listening to the exposure once a day. The other tape, or "session tape," records everything up to the onset of imaginal exposure and also the discussion that follows imaginal exposure.

As will be described in the next chapter, monitoring the client's progress throughout treatment is an important aspect of PE. This is accomplished in part by having him or her complete self-report measures of PTSD and depression every other session. You will review these forms briefly at the beginning of the sessions in which they are completed.

We cannot overemphasize the importance of building a good foundation for treatment that is based on a strong therapeutic alliance and a clear and compelling rationale for treatment. It takes practice to implement a manualized treatment like PE and at the same time provide empathy and support and consistent attention to the therapeutic alliance that is so important in psychotherapy. It is a misconception that following treatment manuals dehumanizes the therapy process, but tailoring the interventions of a treatment manual to the individual client while simultaneously "being a therapist" requires practice and skill.

Structure of Sessions

Session 1 begins by presenting the client with an overview of the treatment program and a general rationale for prolonged exposure. The second part of the session is devoted to collecting information about the trauma, the client's reactions to the trauma, and pretrauma stressful experiences. The Trauma Interview in the appendix was developed to guide you in obtaining information that will be useful in designing the client's treatment program. The session ends with the introduction of breathing retraining. For homework, the client will be instructed to review the Rationale for Treatment, listen to the session audiotape one time before the next session, and practice the breathing retraining on a daily basis. The Breathing Retraining information in the workbook will facilitate the practice of this exercise.

It is a good idea to familiarize yourself with the Trauma Interview before the first session so you are comfortable asking questions about the trauma and the client's history. If you are doing PE with a client whose history you are familiar with, you may not need to ask all of the questions on the Trauma Interview and should modify it accordingly.

Session 2 presents clients with an opportunity to talk in detail about their reactions to the trauma and its effect on them. Common reactions to trauma are discussed in the workbook. This discussion will be didactic and interactive. Next, the rationale for in vivo exposure is presented. Finally, during session 2 the therapist and client together construct a hierarchy of situations or activities and places that the client is avoiding. The client will begin confronting situations for in vivo exposure homework after this session. Session 2 concludes by identifying specific in vivo assignments for that week's homework. The client is also encouraged to continue to practice the breathing exercises, listen to the session audiotape one time before the next session, and read the Common Reactions to Trauma daily.

Session 3 begins with homework review. The therapist then presents the rationale for imaginal exposure, followed by the client's first imaginal revisiting of the trauma memory. During this imaginal exposure, the client is instructed to recount the trauma for 45–60 minutes. This is followed by 15–20 minutes of discussion aimed at helping the client to continue processing thoughts and feelings associated with the trauma. The assigned homework is to listen to the audiotape of the imaginal exposure on a daily basis, listen to the session audiotape one time, and continue with in vivo exposure.

Intermediate Sessions (4–9 or more) consist of homework review, followed by up to 45 minutes of imaginal exposure, 15–20 minutes of postexposure processing of thoughts and feelings, and about 15 minutes of in-depth discussion of the in vivo homework assignments. As treatment advances, the client is encouraged to describe the trauma in much detail during the imaginal revisiting and recounting and to focus progressively more on the most distressing aspects of the trauma experience, or memory "hot spots." In later sessions, as the client improves, imaginal exposure usually becomes shorter, to about 30 minutes.

Session 10 (or Final Session) includes homework review, 20–30 minutes of recounting the trauma memory, discussion of this exposure, with emphasis on how the experience has changed over the course of therapy, and a detailed review of the client's progress in treatment. The final part of the session is devoted to discussing continued application of all that the client has learned in treatment, relapse prevention, and treatment termination.

The following chapter on assessment contains guidelines for selection of clients for whom PE is an appropriate intervention. As previously mentioned, PE is a treatment for PTSD, not a treatment for trauma. Survivors presenting with ongoing trauma-related problems should be assessed thoroughly in order to determine whether or not PE is a suitable treatment.

The client workbook will aid therapists in delivering this treatment. It contains brief information and instructions to clients that follow the format of this manual, as well as blank versions of all forms used during the treatment sessions and for homework assignments. These include forms for creating an exposure hierarchy, conducting imaginal exposure, and tracking imaginal and in vivo exposure homework. Clients will find it extremely helpful to use the workbook to review treatment rationales, record observations during homework exercises, and reinforce what they have learned in session. Clients may photocopy forms from the workbook or download multiple copies from the Treatments *ThatWork*™ Web site at www.oup.com/us/ttw.

Some of the forms used in PE therapy are included in this Therapist Guide. Therapists may photocopy other necessary forms (e.g., exposure homework recording forms, Common Reactions to Trauma information) from the workbook or download multiple copies from the Treatments *ThatWork*™ Web site.

Chapter 2 | *Assessment and Special Considerations in Treating Trauma Survivors*

Who is a good candidate for PE? We begin by answering this question and follow with guidelines for the assessment of trauma survivors with whom you are considering using this therapy. We then discuss some important considerations in using PE with trauma survivors. Finally, we end the chapter with recommendations for assessing and supporting a client's readiness for treatment. PE often results in significant improvement in clients' lives, but it requires a commitment of time, courage, and willingness to learn. Accordingly, with some clients, devoting several sessions to preparation for PE by reviewing the reasons that the client wants to recover from his or her trauma-related difficulties may enhance treatment outcome and retention. Moreover, the ability to tolerate distress and anxiety in order to reclaim a whole and more satisfying life is key, and distress tolerance skills often need to be encouraged and supported by the therapist.

Who Is Appropriate for PE?

Not every trauma survivor needs a trauma-focused treatment like PE. Numerous studies have shown that the mechanisms of natural recovery work quite well for the majority of people who experience a traumatic event (Riggs, Rothbaum, & Foa, 1995; Rothbaum et al., 1992; Kessler et al., 1995). PTSD symptoms and other trauma reactions often surge in the immediate aftermath of a trauma but generally subside over the year following the event, and especially in the first 3 months. Indeed, in order to allow for normal symptom attenuation, we do not assess trauma survivors for our PTSD treatment studies until they are at least 3 months beyond the traumatic event.

If at least a month has passed since the traumatic event and significant levels of PTSD symptoms endure, it is time to consider whether to use PE with your client. On the basis of treating and studying hundreds of trauma survivors, we recommend that PE be considered for use with:

- *Individuals with PTSD and related psychopathology (e.g., depression, chronic anxiety, high levels of anger or shame, axis II disorders) following all types of trauma.* If full diagnostic criteria are not met, the client should still have significant symptoms of the disorder that are distressing and interfering.

- *Individuals with sufficient memory of the traumatic event(s) that they have a narrative:* they can describe the trauma memory (verbally or in writing), and the story has a beginning, middle, and end.

Over the past 20 years, we have progressively minimized the exclusion criteria in our studies in order to evaluate the effectiveness of PE. In doing so, we have learned that PE can be greatly beneficial to PTSD clients with multiple and severe comorbid problems such as major depression or other mood disorders, anxiety disorders, axis II disorders, or alcohol or substance abuse. Although we have widened the gate into our PE treatment programs, we have retained several important and common-sense exclusionary criteria. The presence of any of the following comorbid difficulties should take priority in clinical intervention, and PE should not be implemented until after such intervention has occurred and the condition is stabilized:

- *Imminent threat of suicidal or homicidal behavior.* While current suicidal ideation and even history of suicide gestures or attempts are quite common in our PTSD clients, if the person is currently at high risk for acting on these impulses, the suicidal or homicidal behavior requires clinical attention and stabilization prior to initiation of trauma-focused treatment.

- *Serious self-injurious behavior.* It is also not unusual for PTSD clients to present with histories of cutting or burning or otherwise deliberately injuring themselves. If that type of self-injurious behavior is currently active, PE should be deferred until the person has acquired skills or tools to manage these impulses without acting on them. In our studies, we typically require a period of at least 3 months with no serious self-injurious behavior and a commitment by the clients to use their tools to manage self-harming impulses that may arise. During treatment, we tell clients that they may have urges to harm themselves but that it is not an option during treatment with PE, as they need to learn that they can tolerate their negative emotions and that those emotions will decrease without efforts to escape, avoid, or distract.

■ *Current psychosis.* After years of refraining from using PE with individuals with psychotic disorder diagnoses, we have begun to offer treatment to clients with such history *if they are stabilized on appropriate medications and currently not exhibiting psychotic symptoms.* We have had success with these individuals, but PE has not been systematically studied with this population.

■ *Current high risk of being assaulted (e.g., living with domestic violence).* Many of our clients have lived in dangerous environments that carry a significant risk of negative events and were successfully treated with PE. But if your client is currently in a living situation in which he or she is being beaten, sexually assaulted, or seriously harmed, insuring safety or removal from the dangerous situation should be the focus of intervention. Safety is paramount. PE should be delayed until the person is away from this ongoing violent living situation and the symptoms have had time to stabilize.

■ *Lack of clear memory or insufficient memory of traumatic event(s).* PE should not be employed as a means of helping the client to retrieve or remember a traumatic event. While clients do sometimes remember more details of a trauma through the course of PE, we strongly discourage its use with clients who present with only a "sense" or a vague feeling that they have suffered a trauma that is not remembered.

In addition to these exclusionary criteria, there are several other commonly encountered issues you may need to consider in determining whether to offer a trauma survivor treatment with PE.

Presence of Drug and/or Alcohol Abuse and Dependence

In our early studies, we routinely excluded individuals meeting criteria for abuse and dependence, with the recommendation that they first seek treatment for the drug- and alcohol-related disorders and then return for trauma-focused therapy. We have modified this practice in recent years and now offer PE to PTSD sufferers with current drug and alcohol abuse. However, where appropriate, we frame the substance use as a form of avoidance and strongly encourage the client to curtail or stop the substance use, with the aid of Alcoholics Anonymous or Narcotics Anonymous and other available supports. We monitor the substance abuse throughout treatment and are especially vigilant for its use as a way to decrease or avoid anxiety and other painful feelings.

With the exception of one study, we have refrained from offering PE to clients whose alcohol and/or drug use meets criteria for dependence. But preliminary results of this ongoing study of treatment for clients with comorbid PTSD and alcohol dependence are greatly encouraging in showing that these clients, who are motivated to stop their alcohol use, are able to benefit from PE while receiving concurrent treatment for their alcohol dependence. This suggests that PE may in fact be implemented effectively and successfully for clients with comorbid alcohol and substance dependence along with concurrent treatment focused on the latter. If your client is motivated to stop alcohol or drug use and agrees to engage in concurrent alcohol/substance abuse treatment, then PE may be an appropriate intervention.

Living or Working in a High-Risk Environment

It is reasonable to question whether PE will be effective for someone who lives in a dangerous area or has a hazardous job that carries a significant risk of harm. Unfortunately, examples of this abound: the person living with the threat of terrorist attacks in Israel or war-torn countries, the woman living in an impoverished and violent neighborhood next door to a crack house, and the active-duty marine who will soon be deployed overseas for another tour of duty in a dangerous land. Can PE help someone whose life circumstances make it likely that they may be exposed to more trauma in the future, or even during your treatment of them?

Our experiences in both the United States and abroad have taught us that the answer to this question is yes. If you have determined that the person meets criteria for PTSD, then a significant part of the fear and avoidance the person is experiencing is due to the traumas that happened in the past. While this fear may be fueled by the present-day risk of harm, the reverse is also usually true: the presence of PTSD is likely amplifying their fear and expectations of harm in day-to-day life. To people in these circumstances, we say: "I know that you have a dangerous job (or live in a dangerous place) and that this puts you at risk of more harm. But I also know that you have PTSD because of things that happened in the past, and this disorder causes people to exaggerate estimates of danger in their present life. What I suggest is that you and I work on helping you emotionally process the past trauma so that your PTSD symptoms will diminish, and then we will see what remains. We will do our best to plan your in vivo exposure exercises so that they will be useful to your recovery but will not carry a high risk of harm or danger. I think that when the PTSD symptoms related to this past trauma are reduced, you and I will be better able to address how you can live your life more comfortably given the day-to-day stresses and dangers you may face." This way of thinking about the situation often makes sense and is acceptable to the PTSD client.

Severe Dissociative Symptoms

Clinicians sometimes express reservations about using exposure therapy to treat clients with severe dissociative symptoms or disorders due to concern that the exposure will increase their dissociation. We do not routinely exclude these individuals from our studies, and neither have investigators of other large-scale clinical trials. In considering whether to use PE with such clients, we recommend that you consider the severity of the dissociative symptoms relative to the PTSD. If the client's dissociation experiences outweigh the PTSD-related symptoms in severity and in degree of interference, it may not be possible to effectively implement PE, and the client may not be able to benefit from the treatment.

In such cases, as when other disorders are of primary clinical importance (i.e., severe depression with suicidal risk, severe drug dependence), the more severe or life-threatening disorder should take precedence in clinical intervention.

Presence of Axis II Disorders

We do not exclude clients from PE because of meeting criteria for any personality disorder. In fact, it has been clearly established that many individuals with chronic PTSD do have comorbid Axis II disorders, and our treatment population is consistent with this finding. In two separate studies comparing the outcome of clients with and without personality disorders who were treated for assault-related chronic PTSD, we found no significant differences in improvement in PTSD among the two groups (Feeny, Zoellner, & Foa, 2002; Hembree, Cahill, & Foa, 2004). However, individuals with severe degrees of personality disorder may be excluded from treatment because of safety reasons (e.g., an individual with borderline personality disorder with current serious self-injurious or destructive behavior).

PTSD Accompanied by Prominent Guilt or Shame

Individuals with PTSD sometimes experience prominent guilt or shame, such as the rape survivor who thinks she should have prevented the rape and blames herself for being where she was or for not fighting hard enough, or the soldier who killed someone in the line of duty. Guilt and shame may also be prominent in cases where the client harmed another person accidentally, or in a situation where the person committed a violent act in a moment of extreme stress or rage. Exposure therapy is often effective with these individuals. For example, prolonged exposure using virtual reality of a Virtual Vietnam was effective in a client presenting primarily with guilt (Rothbaum, Ruef, Litz, Han, & Hodges, 2003), and there are case reports in the literature of successful treatment of perpetrators of violence using exposure therapy (e.g., Rogers, Gray, Williams, & Kitchiner, 2000). For PTSD cases where guilt is a primary emotion, we recommend that ample time be devoted to addressing the guilt. Imaginal exposure to the trauma memory will help the client to view the trauma in context and, along with the following processing, will help the client put the events in realistic perspective.

Summary

In summary, regarding who is an appropriate client for treatment with PE, most individuals with PTSD (or severe, clinically significant symptoms) following all types of trauma, who have a clear memory of their traumatic experience(s), are potentially good candidates for PE. Comorbidity of other Axis I and Axis II disorders, as well as multiple life difficulties (e.g., unemployment, financial difficulties, chronic health problems, relationship and family troubles, social isolation, etc.), are extremely common in clients with chronic PTSD, and PE has been successful in the presence of these problems. In general, we recommend that if another disorder is present that is life threatening or otherwise clearly of primary clinical importance, it should be treated prior to initiation of PE.

Keeping in mind the studies showing that PE reduces depression, anxiety, and anger as well as PTSD, its use is warranted in clients with complex trauma histories and complicated clinical presentation. We will return in chapter 8 to the issue of how to maintain focus on emotionally processing traumatic experiences in the face of life struggles and other interference.

Assessment Strategies

A thorough initial evaluation should be conducted to determine whether your trauma survivor is a candidate for PE. In our clinic, this evaluation is used to:

- Obtain a detailed trauma history and determine the index or target trauma (i.e., the trauma that seems to be causing the symptoms and should be the primary focus of attention in treatment)

- Confirm the diagnosis of PTSD (or presence of significant symptoms) and determine its severity

- Assess for the presence of comorbid disorders

- Establish the severity of any other current disorders and whether they will require immediate intervention

Initial evaluation with these aims is conducted with the aid of both interviewer and self-report instruments. We first gather information regarding the history of Criterion A traumatic events and ascertain which of multiple events is currently the most distressing and frequently reexperienced. To diagnose and assess the severity of PTSD, we use the Posttraumatic Symptom Scale–Interview (PSS-I) measure (Foa et al., 1993). The Structured Clinical Interview for *DSM-IV* Axis I Disorders (SCID I; First, Spitzer, Gibbon, & Williams, 1995) or other clinical interviews are used to assess for the presence of other Axis I disorders. Self-report measures include the Posttraumatic Stress Diagnostic Scale (PDS®; Foa, Cashman, Jaycox, & Perry, 1997)* and the Beck Depression Inventory (BDI; Beck, Ward, Mendelson, Mock, & Erbaugh, 1961).

We routinely evaluate clients' symptoms in two ways, and we recommend that you do the same with your clients. First, both interviewer and self-report measures are employed at pre- and posttreatment (and follow-up evaluations) in order to determine overall change in target symptoms. Second, self-report measures (most commonly PDS and BDI) are given to the clients periodically as they progress through therapy. Usually given at the beginning of every other session, these self-report measures permit assessment of change during therapy and are extremely helpful for monitoring progress and giving feedback to the client during treatment.

Special Considerations in Treating Survivors of Interpersonal Violence

When treating a survivor of rape, aggravated assault, or childhood sexual abuse, we need to remain aware that he or she has experienced a major trauma that was caused deliberately by another person. The client

---

*"PDS" is a registered trademark of NCS Pearson, Inc. Pearson Assessments extends a special 50% research discount on the PDS (Posttraumatic Stress Diagnostic Scale) test to readers of this book. If you are interested in conducting research with the PDS test, please contact Pearson Assessments by e-mail at krista.isakson@pearson.com or by phone at 1-800-627-7271, ext. 3313.

is likely to experience extreme fear, and her view of the world may be dominated by pessimism and distrust. Establishing a strong alliance with the client will be crucial in gaining her trust and helping her to emotionally process this experience. In addition, if the trauma is recent, your client may be involved in pressing charges against her assailant, serving a restraining order, or working closely with the police. She may be coping with interpersonal and relationship problems or may need to take care of other people such as family members at a time when she can barely take care of herself. In addition, family members and friends often do not realize how debilitating posttrauma reactions can be. Given all of these factors, it is important to begin PE on a good foundation.

Laying the Groundwork for Treatment

It is very difficult for people with PTSD to confront situations that provoke fear. Usually, prior to seeking professional help, they have tried to face their fears and failed, or have succeeded only a minority of the time, and at great emotional cost. Using PE to help clients overcome their fear successfully is rooted in a foundation that has several cornerstones: a firm grounding in the conceptual model of treatment underlying exposure therapy; a strong, collaborative, therapeutic alliance; a clear and convincing rationale for treatment; and effective implementation of the exposure techniques, which will be addressed throughout this therapist guide.

Conceptual Model

Emotional Processing Theory, the conceptual backbone of PE, was discussed in chapter 1. A clear understanding of this model is extremely important when implementing the therapy. This understanding will aid you in anticipating the course and progress of treatment, guide you in making decisions when presented with choice points or new or unusual problems, and allow you to track the client's progress or determine when your work is done.

Therapeutic Alliance

A critical component of any therapy is a strong therapeutic alliance, and in PE it can be promoted in several ways. First, it is important to acknowledge the client's courage in entering a therapy designed to help her face and overcome strong fears. Clearly align yourself with the client in supporting this effort. Second, be nonjudgmental and comfortable when the client describes her traumatic experience. We have had clients express great relief at being able to tell the therapist their stories and being met with calmness, acceptance, and support. Third, listen closely to the client and use specific examples from her fears and symptoms when presenting education and treatment rationale in the early sessions of therapy. This helps the client to know that she is understood and that you are tailoring this treatment to her unique situation. Fourth, demonstrate knowledge and expertise about PTSD and its treatment. Express confidence in the efficacy of PE and about your ability to implement it effectively. Be active and positive in encouraging the client to attend the sessions, learn these new skills, and practice them during homework. Fifth, be truly collaborative. In constructing an in vivo hierarchy, selecting trauma memories for imaginal exposure, and making decisions about the focus and pace of treatment, you guide the client and make recommendations, but you should always incorporate her judgment and goals. Finally, throughout all stages of therapy, provide abundant support, encouragement, and positive feedback. Good PE therapists are cheerleaders and make clients feel proud of their efforts and accomplishments.

Rationale for Treatment

The vast majority of a PE client's exposure takes place outside of your office and out of your eyesight, so helping the client to really grasp the rationale for treatment is often critical to the success of PE. It can be very difficult to give up avoidance as a strategy for reducing anxiety, and the client must accept the rationale for doing so in order to follow the therapy plan both in and out of session. Being thoroughly grounded in the conceptual model underlying exposure therapy helps you present a convincing rationale. It is also helpful to inform the client that research has shown exposure to be highly effective at reducing the excessive fear that is part of PTSD and that you are knowledgeable about the use of this treatment. We often tell clients that we will push them outside of their comfort zone but not outside of their safety zone.

Challenges of Treating Trauma Survivors

The treatment program described in this therapist guide is time limited and focused on emotionally processing traumatic experiences. It is important to maintain that focus and to keep in mind that the goal of PE is to alleviate PTSD and other trauma-related symptoms. However, the lives of clients with chronic PTSD are often a struggle, with multiple and complex problems. We will return to this issue later in chapter 8, in discussing ways to maintain focus on PE despite ongoing crises and problems in your client's daily life. For some clients, it may be important to help them find appropriate resources if further help is needed. We alert clients to this fact by telling them we are treating only a slice of the pie with PE.

Enhancing Motivation for Treatment

As mentioned above, it is difficult for PTSD sufferers to confront feared and avoided memories and reminders of traumatic experiences. The dropout rate from exposure therapy is no different than that of other active forms of CBT for PTSD (Hembree, Foa, Dorfan, Street, Kowalski, & Tu, 2003), but nonetheless, 20–30% of PTSD clients do terminate treatment prematurely. Avoidance is part of PTSD, and clients often struggle with urges to avoid throughout treatment.

It is helpful to address this with the client right from the onset of therapy. It is also often necessary to revisit it throughout the therapy when a client's avoidance struggles become obstacles to successful outcome. In cases in which the client seems doubtful or uncertain about engaging in the treatment, it may be very beneficial to devote a session or two before initiating PE to discussing the client's motivation for change.

The goals of this discussion are generally to (1) identify areas of the person's life that have been disrupted or are unsatisfying as a result of the trauma; (2) identify potential gains or positive changes that will result from therapy or from reducing PTSD symptoms and related interference; (3) identify and solve likely obstacles to successful therapy (e.g., difficulties attending therapy sessions, finding time to do homework, finding a tape player to listen to audiotapes or the privacy to listen to them, etc.); and (4) if needed, help the client become motivated for therapy.

If the trauma was recent enough that the client can remember life before and after the trauma, assessing the discrepancy between these two times of life can be fruitful. Ask questions like, "How is the PTSD controlling your life? What things that you used to enjoy can you not do anymore or not do without a lot of anxiety?" In pursuing this line of questioning, you may identify the changes your client hopes to achieve, and the life he wants to reclaim, through PE.

Other useful areas to explore:

- "Are there things that your friends or other people are able to do that you do not do at the present time?"

- "What would you like to change in your life now? What do you wish you could do at the end of therapy or 6 months from now?"

- "Have you tried to get help for this in the past? What was it like? Did it help you? If not, why not? What made it difficult for you? If you did not complete treatment, what made you decide to stop?"

- "Some people going through PE feel worse before they feel better, and their symptoms may increase before heading down. Given what you know about yourself, if this happens, how will it be for you? Is there anything I can do to help you tolerate this temporary worsening?

- "As we have discussed, PE requires time and effort. The homework is an important part of the process. Is there anything that may hinder your being able to do this?"

- "Sometimes there are aspects of people's lives that actually change for the *better* after a trauma. Is this true for you, and, if so, what do you feel you have gained from experiencing the trauma?"

■ "Although PE is often really beneficial in helping people get their lives back, it also can be stressful and may at times be time-intensive and demanding. Let us think together whether the effort of therapy is in fact worthwhile for you. What will happen in your life if you don't work on these problems?"

Tips for the Trauma Therapist: How Do You Care for Yourself?

Our experience as trainers and supervisors has taught us that even experienced therapists are at times concerned about using PE procedures with highly distressed PTSD clients. As any therapist who has listened to a painful and horrifying experience can attest, helping a client to emotionally process traumatic events can be challenging and emotionally difficult. In order to conduct PE, therapists sometimes need to develop or increase their own tolerance for client distress. These procedures trigger an intense emotional response; indeed, this is the purpose of the work. How can you cope with this reaction in your client? How do you manage your own reaction to hearing such graphic and painful experiences?

First, let the model guide you. At the same time that we are helping clients to learn that intense anxiety and emotional engagement with painful memories cannot hurt them as the original trauma did and that anxiety does not last indefinitely, we also have to trust this fact ourselves. Developing tolerance for client distress requires that the *therapist* accept the rationale for treatment, and especially the idea that memories cannot hurt the client. It is typical for the therapist to habituate to the trauma memory along with the client over the course of the treatment.

Nonetheless, conducting PE is at times emotionally challenging and replete with difficult choices for the therapist. The internal dialogue of a trauma therapist is full of questions: "Do I stop the imaginal exposure now because of how upset she is? What if this makes her more depressed? What if she keeps feeling this way when she's not in my office? Is this a realistically safe situation she is avoiding?" Allowing the treatment model to guide these decisions both assists in making the decisions and leads to decisions well grounded in the available research. Keep in mind that even though emotional processing is painful work, for most clients it is quite beneficial. Remind *yourself* of this as often as you do the client.

Decision making should also be guided by the goal of promoting the client's sense of control. While our job is to make recommendations, *never* try to compel or pressure unwilling clients to do exposures. A difficult decision we sometimes have to face is whether to encourage the client to continue therapy or to help her terminate therapy if she is not ready to confront trauma-related fears and avoidance. If the client is not ready for trauma-focused treatment, it is better to have her stop, rather than have her fail to get better and leave treatment believing that PE did not and cannot decrease her symptoms, or that she somehow failed the treatment. We will often tell the client that PE is quite effective for most people, so we would rather stop now and invite her to come back when she is ready since she now knows what will be required.

Supervision with an expert or consultation with peers can be beneficial and can provide technical and emotional support. Ideally, have a team or supervision group that meets regularly to discuss trauma treatment cases. Regular consultation provides opportunities for input from colleagues regarding difficult decisions about how to proceed with these often complex and challenging cases.

Chapter 3 | *Session 1*

(Corresponds to chapter 3 of the workbook)

Materials Needed

- Rationale for Treatment

- Trauma Interview

- Breathing retraining technique

- Two audiotapes to record session and breathing retraining exercise

Session Outline

- Present an overview of the program (25–30 minutes)

- Discuss the treatment procedures that will be used in the program

- Explain that the focus of the program is on PTSD symptoms

- Collect information relevant to the trauma using the Trauma Interview (45 minutes)

- Introduce breathing retraining (10–15 minutes)

- Assign homework (5 minutes)

Present Overview of Program and Treatment Procedures Used (25–30 minutes)

In the beginning of this first PE session, you will present the client with an overall rationale for PE and will describe the main tools of the therapy: imaginal and in vivo exposure. Although delivering rationales is didactic, try to make this discussion interactive by asking the client questions or inviting him to share his experiences or thoughts. Ensure that the client understands the rationale by inviting him to ask questions.

Some clients comment that they have tried and failed to face fears or that they did face them but their anxiety did not diminish. Some just cannot picture themselves stopping their avoidance or being strong enough to visualize and describe traumatic memories. For clients who are uncertain about the efficacy of treatment or their ability to benefit from it, you should aim to help them see that the approach at least makes sense and that it will be different from how they have approached it in the past.

Introduce the client to the treatment program using the following introduction dialogue:

> Today is our first session together, and I would like to spend most of the session getting to know each other and asking you some questions about your past experiences and feelings. But first I will explain the goals of the program to you and talk with you about the techniques that you will be learning when we work together.

Explain to the client that the treatment program consists usually of 10 to 12 90-minute sessions, but occasionally it can take up to 15 sessions in total.

Continue the introduction using the following script:

> We will meet once or twice per week, so the therapy will be completed in about two or three months. In this program, we are going to focus on the fears that you are experiencing and your difficulty coping, both of which are directly related to your traumatic experience(s). Although many times posttrauma reactions gradually decline with time, for many survivors like you, some of these symptoms endure and continue to cause marked distress. It is helpful in your recovery process to understand what maintains posttrauma difficulties.
>
> A major factor is **avoidance**. There are two ways that people avoid dealing with trauma reminders. The first is trying to push away memories, thoughts, and feelings about the trauma. The second is escaping or avoiding situations, places, people, and objects that cause distress and fear because they are similar to the trauma or are re-

minders of the trauma. However, while the strategy of avoiding trauma-related thoughts and situations works in the short run, it actually prolongs the posttrauma reactions and prevents you from getting over your trauma-related difficulties. Can you think of things that you have avoided since the trauma?

Because avoiding thoughts about the trauma and situations that remind you of the trauma maintains your PTSD, the treatment that you will receive aims to help you stop avoidance and instead encourages you to confront trauma-related thoughts and situations. The treatment includes two types of confrontations or exposures. The first one is called **imaginal exposure,** in which we will ask you to revisit the traumatic experience in your imagination and recount the trauma aloud. Imaginal exposure aims to enhance your ability to process the traumatic memory by asking you to recount the memory repeatedly during the sessions. We have found that repeated and prolonged (up to 45 minutes) imaginal exposure to the traumatic memory is very effective in reducing trauma-related symptoms and helping you get new perspective and meaning about what happened before, during, and after the traumatic event.

The second type of exposure is called **in vivo exposure,** which just means confronting situations you avoid "in real life." Here we will ask you to gradually approach situations that you have been avoiding because they remind you of the trauma, directly or indirectly (e.g., driving a car, walking alone in safe place, or lighting a fire in the fireplace). In vivo exposure has been found very effective in reducing excessive fears and avoidance after a trauma. For example, if you avoid trauma-related situations that are objectively safe, you do not give yourself the opportunity to get over your fear of these situations. This is because until you confront these situations, you may continue to believe that they are dangerous, or that you will not be able handle them, or that your anxiety in these situations will remain indefinitely. However, if you confront these situations in a gradual, systematic way, you will find out that they are not actually dangerous, that you can handle them, and that your anxiety will diminish with repeated, prolonged confrontations. Does the idea of exposure make sense to you?

A second factor that maintains your posttrauma reactions is **the presence of unhelpful, disturbing thoughts and beliefs**. These disturbing *beliefs are about the world in general, other people, yourself, and your reaction to the trauma. As a result of trauma, many people adopt the belief that the world is extremely dangerous. Therefore, even objectively safe situations are viewed as dangerous. Also, immediately after the trauma, many people adopt the view that they are incompetent and unable to cope, even with normal daily stresses. Trauma survivors may also blame themselves for the trauma and put themselves down because they are having difficulty coping after it. Resuming daily activities and not avoiding trauma reminders helps survivors realize that most of the time the world is safe and that most of the time they are competent. However, avoiding trauma reminders and developing PTSD often makes survivors continue to believe that the world is extremely dangerous and that they are incompetent and unable to cope. Do you feel this way about yourself?*

How do these excessively negative and unrealistic thoughts and beliefs about the world and about yourself maintain your posttrauma reactions? If you believe that the world is dangerous, you will continue to avoid even safe situations. Similarly, if you believe that the trauma is your fault, you are likely to blame yourself and feel incompetent, and this will interfere with your ability to get back to your life before the trauma. Likewise, if you believe that experiencing flashbacks is a sign that you are losing control, you may try very hard to push the memories out of your mind. However, the more you try to push these memories away, the more they will intrude on your mind and the less control you will actually have over the memories.

These disturbing thoughts and beliefs may be triggered during the repeated imaginal and in vivo exposures. But the recounting of the traumatic event will give you the opportunity to gain a new, more realistic perspective about what happened and what it means to you now and to help you get over your PTSD symptoms. We're going to try to make sense of a senseless situation, to give you a way to think about it.

We are going to work very hard together during the next few weeks to help you get on with your life. Our work will be intensive, and you may find that you are experiencing discomfort as we confront your trauma reminders. I want you to know that I would be happy to talk with you between sessions if you feel that it would be helpful to you. Do you have any questions that you would like to ask me about the treatment program or information that I have just given to you?

What I would like to do for the rest of the session is talk with you about some of your experiences before the trauma and your reactions to the trauma. To do this I am going to use a standardized interview. At the end of session I will teach you a skill called breathing retraining to help you breathe in a calming way.

Information Gathering (45 minutes)

Use the Trauma Interview in appendix A to collect general information about the immediate presenting problems, the client's functioning, the traumatic experience(s), physical and mental health since the trauma, social support, and use of alcohol and drugs. The Trauma Interview is also designed to aid in the identification of the "target trauma," or the one that will be the focus of treatment, for clients who present with a history of multiple traumatic events.

Asking specific and directive questions about topics may elicit emotional responses from the client. However, if a particular topic provokes great discomfort, use your judgment in deciding whether to focus on this area at greater length or to postpone the questioning until a later time. When you make this decision, it is important that you take into account the expressed needs and wishes of the client. When you get to the trauma section, it is best to ask the client to give you a brief summary of what occurred and to remind him that you will talk about it in more detail during the therapy.

Proceed with the Trauma Interview.

Breathing Retraining (10–15 minutes)

Introduce the client to breathing retraining at the end of the first session in order to give him a tool to practice at home in the coming week. The rationale for this technique is as follows:

Very often, when people become frightened or upset, they feel like they need more air and may therefore breathe fast or hyperventilate. Hyperventilation, however, does not have a calming effect. In fact it generates anxious feelings. Unless we are preparing for fighting or fleeing from real danger, we often don't need as much air as we are taking in. When we hyperventilate and take in more air, it signals our bodies to prepare for fighting or fleeing and to keep it fueled with oxygen. This is similar to a runner taking deep breaths to fuel the body with oxygen before a race and continuing to breathe deeply and quickly throughout the race. Hyperventilating also produces bodily reactions that resemble fear. These bodily reactions, in turn, can make us more afraid. Usually, though, when we hyperventilate, we are tricking our bodies. And what we really need to do is to slow down our breathing and take in less air. So learning to breathe slowly and calmly provides a useful tool for reducing stress or tension.

*Most of us realize that our breathing also affects the way that we feel. For example, when we are upset, people may tell us to take a deep breath and calm down. Again, however, we think that it is not really **deep** breathing that helps, but **slow** breathing. In order to calm down or relax one should take normal breaths and exhale slowly. It is exhalation that is associated with relaxation, not inhalation. Also, it can be helpful to associate your exhalation with a word that has a calming or relaxing effect. So while you exhale, say the words "calm" or "relax" silently to yourself very slowly. Like this: c-a-a-a-a-a-l-m.*

When suggesting a cue word for relaxation, ask the client if he has a preference for a specific word. Most people find the words *calm* or *relax* helpful. Model for the client how to inhale and exhale slowly through the nose, and then ask the client to perform the exercise according to the following instructions:

In addition to concentrating on slow exhalation while saying "calm" to yourself, I want you to do one other thing to slow down your breathing. After you finish exhaling, and when your lungs are empty of air, I'd like you to pause for a count of 3 or 4 seconds before inhaling again. So it will go like this: "Inhale (a normal breath . . . exhale (very slowly) . . . Caaaaaaaaallllllmmmmm . . . hold 1 . . . 2 . . . 3 . . . 4 . . . Inhale (normal breath) . . . exhale," etc.

After practicing for a few respiratory cycles to get the client accustomed to the breathing pattern, repeat the entire breathing sequence 10–15 times, while making a 3-minute tape of your voice leading the client through these breathing exercises: *"Inhale . . . exhale . . . Caaaaaallllmmm . . . hold 1 . . . 2 . . . 3 . . . 4 . . . inhale . . . exhale . . . Caaaaaallllmmm,"* etc. Thus while the client is exhaling slowly, you will say the word "calm" aloud, dragging it out very slowly, to a count of 4 seconds. The practice tape the client will bring home contains 3 minutes of your voice guiding him through the breathing at a slow pace. At this point, instruct the client to review the Breathing Retraining information in the workbook.

Homework (5 minutes)

✎ Instruct client to practice breathing retraining for 10 minutes, 3 times a day. Suggest that clients use the breathing retraining when they feel particularly tense or distressed throughout the day or to help relax at night before going to sleep.

✎ Ask client to listen to the audiotape of session one time.

✎ Instruct client to read the Rationale for Treatment in the workbook.

✎ Remind client to come early to next session to complete self-report forms.

Chapter 4 | *Session 2*

(Corresponds to chapter 4 of the workbook)

Materials Needed

■ Self-report scales for measuring PTSD and depression*

■ In Vivo Exposure Hierarchy

■ In Vivo Exposure Homework Recording Form

■ Audiotape to record session

Session Outline

■ Review homework (5–10 minutes)

■ Present agenda for session (3 minutes)

■ Educate client about PTSD symptoms by discussing common reactions to trauma (25–30 minutes)

■ Discuss the rationale for exposure with emphasis on in vivo (10 minutes)

■ Introduce the Subjective Unit of Discomfort Scale (SUDS) (5 minutes)

■ Construct in vivo hierarchy (20 minutes)

---

*As discussed in chapter 2, we recommend that you regularly monitor clients' PTSD and depression symptoms by having them complete self-report measures at the beginning of every other session of PE (e.g., sessions 2, 4, 6, 8). We use the PTSD symptom section of the Posttraumatic Stress Diagnostic Scale (PDS®) and the Beck Depression Inventory (BDI) to do so. This permits assessment of change during therapy and is extremely helpful for monitoring progress and giving feedback to clients during treatment.

- Select in vivo assignments for homework (5 minutes)

- Assign homework (10 minutes)

Overview

After this session, clients will begin in vivo exposure practice. For most clients, the in vivo exposures cannot be easily conducted during sessions, and the in vivo exposure practices are done between sessions as homework exercises. However, sometimes a client's in vivo exposure includes items that can be accomplished during the therapy session. Examples are exposure items such as greeting men or making eye contact with them (if there are any men in the clinic or vicinity), lying on one's back with eyes closed, sitting in a waiting room with unfamiliar people, sitting at a table in a cafeteria by oneself or with one's back to others, etc. These situations may be first attempted in the latter part of the therapy session with the therapist's support, if it seems useful. The client will then continue to practice that particular exposure for homework. The last 10–15 minutes of each session will focus on planning the upcoming in vivo exposure.

Homework Review (5–10 minutes)

At the beginning of the session, ask the client how she has been doing in the past week and what her reactions were to the first session. If the client has completed the PDS® and BDI just prior to the session as recommended, review the client's symptoms quickly. These self-report measures will allow you to give the client feedback on changes that may occur in symptoms of depression and PTSD as treatment progresses. Ask the client how often she used the breathing retraining and how useful she found the technique during the last week. Discuss her reactions to listening to the audiotape of the session, and ask if she has any questions about the Rationale for Treatment. Altogether, spend about 10 minutes reviewing homework and talking about how the client has been doing.

Set Agenda (3 minutes)

Present the client with the agenda for the session by telling her that you are first going to discuss the usual/common reactions that people have to trauma as well as her experience of these reactions. Explain to her that you will also review the rationale for in vivo exposure and work together to construct a list of situations that are upsetting and that she has been avoiding.

Discussion about the Common Reactions to Trauma (25–30 minutes)

Information for Therapists

This part of the session will focus on educating the client about common reactions to trauma. It is intended to be an interactive dialogue between you and the client. Avoid lecturing the client; instead, encourage her to discuss her feelings, thoughts, and behaviors since the trauma.

The discussion of common reactions to trauma has several aims:

- Elicit from the client her own experience of PTSD symptoms and related problems while providing education.

- Validate and normalize the client's experience in the context of trauma and PTSD. Many clients are helped tremendously by being able to understand their behavior and reactions in relation to the trauma they have experienced.

- Instill hope: help the client to realize that many of her distressing symptoms are directly related to the PTSD and that much of this may improve as a function of treatment.

A case example of the interactive approach to present common reactions to trauma is provided at the end of this section. Read the example before the session to acquaint yourself with the style of dialogue.

Proceed with the discussion of your client's PTSD symptoms:

1. Discuss the specific *DSM-IV-TR* PTSD symptoms of reexperiencing, avoidance, emotional numbing, and hyperarousal, using the descriptions provided here (or the Common Reactions to Trauma information in the workbook).

2. Discuss the secondary symptoms of guilt and shame, low self-esteem, sense of loss of control, loss of interest in physical intimacy, and reactivation of past traumatic memories after a trauma.

3. Explain the relationships among the traumatic event, distressing feelings, physiological reactions, disturbing thoughts, and avoidance responses.

Important: Clients whose trauma occurred a long time ago (e.g., an adult survivor of childhood sexual or physical abuse, or a veteran of a long-ago war) might not have a sense of their life before the trauma. They may not recognize that they refrain from doing certain things because they avoid trauma reminders. They may view their avoidance behaviors as preferences, habits, or patterns of living that prevent them from being uncomfortable. Some clients tell us, "This is just the way I have always been." In these cases, you will need to tailor this discussion to the client's particular situation, the length of time since the trauma occurred, and her perceptions.

Presentation to Client

Use the following introduction to begin the discussion about common reactions to a traumatic experience. Use probe questions during the discussion of trauma reactions to stimulate discussion of your client's specific reactions.

A trauma is an emotional shock. I know that the [name the specific incident] has affected you greatly. Today, I want to discuss with you the common reactions of people who have undergone a severe trauma. Although each person responds in his or her own unique way, you may find that you have experienced many of these reactions.

Continue the discussion using the following script as a guide.

1. The primary reactions people experience after a trauma are fear and anxiety. Are you feeling fearful, tense, or anxious?

Encourage the client to respond.

Sometimes your feeling of anxiety may be a result of being reminded of the trauma; at other times the anxiety may feel to you as if it comes out of the blue. Do you notice that you are more fearful at certain times than others?

Encourage the client to respond.

The feelings of anxiety and fear that you are experiencing can be understood as reactions to a dangerous and life-threatening situation. You may experience changes in your body, your feelings, and your thoughts because your view of the world and your perceptions about your safety have changed as a result of the trauma.

Certain triggers and cues may remind you of the trauma and activate your fears. These triggers may be certain times of the day, certain places, particular activities, strangers approaching you, a certain smell, or a noise. Have you noticed specific triggers that remind you of the trauma?

Encourage clients to share their own relevant experiences.

Typically, after a trauma, fear and anxiety are experienced in two primary ways: (a) continuing to reexperience memories of the trauma; (b) feeling aroused, easily startled, and jumpy. How has this been for you?

Encourage clients to share their own relevant experiences.

2. People who have been traumatized also reexperience the trauma. You may find that you are having flashbacks when visual pictures of some aspect of the incident suddenly pop into your mind. Are you having flashbacks? What is this experience like for you?

Encourage clients to share their own relevant experiences.

Sometimes the flashback may be so vivid that you might feel as if the trauma is actually occurring again. These experiences are intrusive and you probably feel that you don't have any control over what you are feeling, thinking, and experiencing during the day or at night.

Sometimes these flashbacks are triggered by external events and often they appear to come out of nowhere.

You may also find that you are reexperiencing the trauma through nightmares. Have you been having nightmares?

Encourage clients to share their own relevant experiences.

What changes do you notice in your body when you suddenly wake up from a nightmare?

You may also reexperience the trauma emotionally or cognitively without having a flashback or nightmare. Have you been having distressing thoughts and feelings about what happened to you?

3. You may also find that you are having trouble concentrating. This is another common experience that results from a trauma.

Are you having any trouble reading, following a conversation, or remembering something that someone told you? What is this like for you?

It is frustrating and upsetting to be unable to concentrate, remember, and pay attention to what is going on around you. This experience also leads to a feeling that you are not in control of your mind or a feeling that you are going crazy. Difficulties concentrating are sometimes due to intrusive and distressing feelings and memories about the trauma. At other times, it may seem to be not connected at all, but it is still part of the hyperarousal symptoms that are part of PTSD.

4. Other common reactions to trauma are arousal, agitation, feeling jittery, feeling overly alert, trembling, being easily startled, and having trouble sleeping. Sometimes feeling tense and jumpy all the time may also lead to feelings of irritability, especially if you are not getting enough sleep.

Have you noticed that your body is experiencing any of these changes since the trauma? Are there times when you feel panic? What happens to your body? Do you sweat? Does your heart race? Are you especially watchful and easily startled?

Encourage clients to share their own relevant experiences.

5. You may find that you are physically, emotionally, or cognitively avoiding people, places, or things that remind you of the trauma. Avoidance is a strategy to protect yourself from situations you feel have become dangerous and from thoughts and feelings that are overwhelming and distressing.

Are you unable to go certain places or do certain things as a result of the trauma? Have you been making efforts to avoid thoughts or feelings associated with the trauma? How do you do that?

What kinds of things do you find yourself doing to try to forget what happened to you?

Sometimes the desire to avoid memories and feelings about the trauma may be so intense that you might find you have forgotten important aspects of what happened during the trauma.

Are there any parts of the trauma that you cannot remember or gaps of time that you cannot account for?

Another experience you may have from avoiding painful feelings and thoughts about the trauma is emotional numbness.

Do you have this experience of feeling numb, empty, or detached from your environment? Have you found that you have lost interest in things that once were pleasurable to you? Do you feel detached and cut off from other people since the trauma?

6. Other common reactions to trauma are sadness and a sense of feeling down or depressed. You may have feelings of hopelessness and despair, frequent crying spells, and sometimes even thoughts of hurting yourself and suicide. Trauma survivors often feel a sense of grief for what they have lost or for who they were before the trauma occurred. A loss of interest in the people and activities that you once found pleasurable is often associated with a trauma. Nothing may seem fun to you any more. You may also feel that life isn't worth living and plans that you had made for the future do not seem important any longer.

Have you been feeling sad or depressed? Are you tearful? Are you feeling stuck or hopeless? Are you having any feelings or ideas that life is not worth living or that you would be better off dead? (See Suicide Assessment box.)

Suicide Assessment

If the client has suicidal ideation, discontinue the discussion of the common reactions to trauma and conduct a suicide assessment. Ask the client about her thoughts, urges, feelings, fantasies, and plans she may have to harm herself. Inquire if she has ever thought about or planned to hurt herself in the past. If she has, ask her what she planned or what she did. Ask her if she has any intention of carrying out these plans. You may want to ask the client to sign an agreement to contact you, a hospital emergency room, or another mental health professional if she has thoughts or plans to harm herself. As discussed in chapter 2, when clients present with current high risk of suicidal behavior, this should take precedence in intervention, and PE can be resumed after these symptoms have been addressed and treated.

7. During the trauma, you felt threatened. You may have felt as if you had no control over your feelings, your body, and your life. Sometimes the feelings of loss of control may be so intense that you may feel as if you are "going crazy" or "losing it."

Have you had this experience since the trauma? What is that like for you?

8. Feelings of guilt and shame may be present. Guilt and shame may be related to something you did or did not do to survive the trauma. It is common to second guess your reactions and blame yourself for what you did or did not do.

Are you blaming yourself for the trauma? Do you feel that if you had or had not done something, the traumatic experience could have been avoided? Are there any people that you are avoiding talking to or things that you are avoiding doing because you feel guilty or ashamed?

Blame can also come from society, friends, family, and acquaintances because many times people place responsibility on the person who has been hurt and victimized.

Has anyone blamed you for the trauma? What do you think about that?

9. A feeling of anger is also a very common reaction to trauma. The anger often is associated with a strong sense of unfairness or injustice that you were a victim of such a terrible experience. While anger may be mostly directed at a specific cause of the trauma, feelings of anger may be also stirred up in the presence of people who in some way remind you of the event.

Are you feeling particularly angry or aggressive? Do you find that you are having angry outbursts or that you are more snappy than usual with people? Is this different from the way you felt before the trauma?

How do these feelings affect you or other people?

Sometimes you may find that you are so angry that you want to hit someone or swear. If you are not used to feeling angry you may not recognize or know how to handle these angry feelings.

Many people also direct the anger toward themselves for something that they did or did not do during the trauma. These feelings of anger directed at the self may lead to feelings of blame, guilt, helplessness, and depression.

Many people also find that they are experiencing anger and irritability toward those people that they love the most: family, friends, their partners, and their children. Has this been happening to you?

Sometimes you might lose your temper with the people who are most dear to you. This may be confusing, since you may not understand why you are angry and irritable with those you care about most. While closeness with others may feel good, it also increases the opportunity for feelings of intimacy, dependency, vulnerability and helplessness. Having those feelings may make you feel angry and irritable because they remind you of the trauma.

10. Self-image can also suffer as a result of a trauma. You may tell yourself, "I am a bad person and bad things happen to me," or "If I had not been so weak or stupid, this would not have happened to me," or "I should have been tougher."

Are you having any negative thoughts about yourself since the trauma? What kinds of things do you find yourself saying or thinking about your feelings or the way you are coping?

11. It is not unusual to have disruptions in relationships with other people after a traumatic experience. This disruption is in part a result of feeling sad, frightened, and angry. In order to cope with these negative feelings, you may withdraw from others or not participate in the activities that you once did. You may also find that the people you love the most and expect to be the most supportive are not.

Has this been a problem for you? Have you noticed that you are having difficulties getting along with other people?

It is common for people to experience anger, anguish, and guilt when people they love are hurt. You may find that your friends and family, especially your partner, may have difficulty hearing about your trauma and may have serious reactions to it. It is important that you get support for what you are going through and that you understand that some of the people around you might be going through a crisis too.

At the same time, the support of your family and friends plays an important role in your recovery. It is important to talk to people who you feel can support you and understand your feelings.

12. After a trauma, it is not unusual to experience a loss of interest in physical affection and sexual relations. There are various reasons for this. For example, it is very common for people who are depressed and have not been traumatized to experience a loss of interest in their sexual drive. Also, disinterest in or fear of physical and sexual relations is extremely common in those who have been traumatized.

Are you experiencing any loss of interest in sexual relations? Have you experienced any frightening feelings, thoughts, or flashbacks during physical contact with anyone?

You may feel uncomfortable being emotionally and sexually intimate with someone because this experience may bring back your feelings of vulnerability during the trauma. In fact, you may have flashbacks or intensely distressing feelings when you are having sexual or physical contact.

13. As a result of a recent trauma, you may be reminded of your past experiences. Once a negative experience comes to your mind, it tends to provoke memories of other negative experiences. This is the normal way your memory works. For this reason, after the trauma, you may recall many negative feelings about a past trauma that you had forgotten. These memories may be as disturbing to you as the memories of the recent trauma.

It may be difficult for you to think of any other situations or experiences that are not negative. In fact, it may be very difficult to believe that you will ever feel happy or have pleasant experiences again. But you will. In fact, you will find that it is possible for you to put these negative experiences behind you, and you will start to remember more positive memories. These positive memories will trigger more positive recollections and eventually you will gain a more balanced view of your life.

Have you suddenly remembered upsetting experiences that you had before the recent event?

14. Finally, some people increase their use of alcohol or other substances after a trauma. There is nothing wrong with responsible drinking, but if your use of alcohol or drugs has increased as a result of your traumatic experience, it can slow down your recovery and cause problems of its own.

Have you been drinking alcohol or using other substances? Has this increased significantly since the trauma? Do you notice if there are certain times that you tend to drink more than other times?

Some of these common reactions to trauma are connected with each other. For some people, having a flashback may increase their concern about losing control of their lives and may even intensify their fears. In other words, the responses to being traumatized often interact with one another and cause the overall response to be more intense. As you become aware of the changes you have gone through since the trauma and as you process these experiences during treatment, the symptoms should become less distressing.

After the discussion, ask the client to review the Common Reactions to Trauma information in the workbook as part of homework. If appropriate, suggest that the client share the information with significant others.

Case Example: Presenting Common Reactions to Trauma

▨ *In the following example, where T represents the therapist and C represents the client, we present a sample dialogue of the Common Reactions to Trauma discussion. For brevity, only 5 of the 14 reactions listed above are presented in this illustration.*

Mary is a 40-year-old woman who works as an administrative assistant in a private corporation. Mary lives with her husband and two children in the suburbs. She went to the grocery store at 6 a.m. and was forced into her car by a young white male at knifepoint. He raped her in her car while parked in the lot of the grocery store. The therapist interviewed her 4 months after she had been raped.

During the initial interview, Mary reported anxiety, sleeping difficulties, flashbacks, nervousness, and loss of appetite. Mary also was unable to get into her car or go to work and reported extreme irritability with her family. ▨

T: I know that you are feeling very uncomfortable and upset now, but I want you to know that the symptoms you are experiencing are common reactions to a traumatic event. Talking today about the kinds of responses people often experience to a trauma such as you've had will help you to understand better what you've been experiencing.

C: I feel like my life is turned upside down and I will never be the same. I can't concentrate on anything and I am afraid to go to work. I'm worried that I am going to lose my job because I tried to go back recently, but I couldn't handle it and went out again.

T: That is really a frightening feeling, isn't it? Why don't we talk a little bit more about reactions to trauma. What I would like us to do, as we review each type of reaction, is to discuss what you are experiencing. You said you've noticed that you are having difficulties concentrating since the assault?

C: Yeah . . . I feel very spaced out and like I can't pay attention to anything.

T: When you can't concentrate, what is happening?

C: I just keep having pictures of the rape go through my mind over and over. I can't get rid of them.

T: It is frustrating and upsetting to be unable to concentrate, remember, and pay attention to what is going on around you. The images that pop into your head are called reexperiencing symptoms and usually interrupt your ability to concentrate. They also may make you feel extremely anxious. Can you give examples of specific situations when you have these images?

C: Yes. Every time I look at my car I see his face and the knife in his hand. I will never be able to drive that car again. Yesterday my husband drove me to the grocery store and I couldn't get out of his car. He says I am overreacting.

T: Sometimes it seems that the reexperiencing symptoms—images, thoughts, or flashbacks—come out of nowhere, but often they are triggered by external events or objects, such as your car, parking lots, the grocery store, and seeing someone who resembles the assailant. Another way that you can reexperience the trauma is through nightmares. Have you been having any nightmares?

C: Most nights I can't even get to sleep. My husband thinks I am crazy because I want to sleep with the light on. I fall asleep toward morning and usually only sleep an hour or two before I wake up again and I can't get back to sleep.

T: Many women tell us that after an assault they need to sleep with the light on to help them feel safer. One of the things that you may wish to do is to discuss these reactions with your husband or give him this information to read so that he has a better understanding that what you are going through is a common reaction to trauma. Are you experiencing any bad dreams once you fall asleep?

C: Yeah, but they are not about the assault. They are just violent and upsetting dreams.

T: Many women report similar experiences after they have been assaulted. You may have nightmares about the trauma that are violent in nature but not specific to the assault. This is all a part of the reexperiencing that people who are survivors of a traumatic event go through. Have you noticed that your body is experiencing any changes?

C: Do you mean like when my heart starts beating rapidly?

T: Exactly. Are there any other sensations that you experience?

C: I feel very jittery and it is a feeling of panic. It is very difficult for me to describe. It is like I am super-alert.

T: You described that very well. In fact, these are the types of symptoms that people often report after a trauma. These are the body's reactions to feeling very anxious and fearful.

C: I can understand my feeling that way during the assault but why do I keep feeling that way over and over again?

T: As a result of the trauma, you have realized that there is danger in the world and you want to be prepared for it. Your body is in a constant state of preparedness and arousal so you can feel pumped and ready to respond at any moment. Another reason that you are feeling aroused or jumpy all of the time is because there are triggers or reminders of the trauma. We have already talked about a few—your car, parking lots, grocery stores, someone who looks like the assailant—but there are probably other triggers that are more subtle, such as when someone comes up behind you, when your husband puts his arm around you, when you see a car that looks like yours, or when you see strangers. Triggers or reminders do not have to be just external events or objects. You may experience feeling cold and chilly and that may remind you of the way you felt during the assault. So feeling cold and chilly becomes a trigger for reactions of fear and anxiety. Are there any other experiences that you have had that reminded you of the assault?

C: Yes, many things seem to remind me of it. For that reason, I feel like I just want to hide away, not talk about it, and not deal with anyone or anything. I just want to be alone—sometimes even away from my family.

T: A natural response to trauma is to want to avoid contact with reminders of the trauma. You may find that you are avoidant of many things—people, places, or anything that reminds you of the trauma. Avoidance is a strategy to protect yourself from situations that you feel have become or could become dangerous and from thoughts and feelings that are overwhelming and distressing to you. You mentioned earlier that you are unable to go grocery shopping or even sit in your car.

Are there any other places, people, or situations that you are avoiding because they remind you of the assault?

C: No, not really.

T: You said that you tried to return to work?

C: Yes, but I just couldn't handle it—the drive, feeling so jumpy and not being able to think straight—it was just overwhelming.

T: That makes sense to me, given what you've experienced. I think that as you understand these reactions better, and we work together to help you to recover from this rape, your symptoms will gradually decrease. You will feel better able to handle the challenges of going back to work. I'm glad that you came in for help.

Presentation of In Vivo Exposure

Rationale (10 minutes)

Present the client with the following rationale for in vivo exposure:

> In our first session we talked about the imaginal and in vivo exposure procedures and why we think they are helpful in recovering from the types of symptoms we just discussed. Today we will review the rationale for in vivo exposure and why confronting trauma-related situations that you want to avoid will help you overcome your PTSD. We will then begin to construct a list of situations that you have been avoiding and that would be suitable for in vivo exposure.

> You recall that it is quite common for people to want to escape or avoid memories, situations, thoughts, and feelings that are painful and distressing. However, while this avoidance of painful or anxiety-arousing experiences works in the short run, what does it do in the long run?

If the client cannot give an appropriate answer, remind her that avoidance prolongs posttrauma reactions and prevents recovery from PTSD.

You may also want to elicit examples of the client's avoidance based on the previous discussion of common reactions.

> *It is for this reason that part of the program involves helping you to confront these trauma-related situations that you are avoiding now. There are several ways in which in vivo exposure will help you overcome your PTSD symptoms.* **First**, *you have developed a habit of reducing anxiety through avoiding situations that cause you to feel anxious or scared. For example, you are at home and you discover that you ran out of milk. You say to yourself: "It does not make sense to wait until my husband returns from work. I should go the supermarket myself."' As you contemplate this thought you begin to feel very anxious. Then you say to yourself: "I can wait for my husband to come home and shop for the milk." Immediately after you make the decision not to go shopping, your anxiety decreases and you feel better. Each time you reduce your anxiety by avoidance, your habit of avoiding gets stronger and stronger. In vivo exposure, that is, systematically confronting feared situations that you now avoid, will help you overcome your habit of reducing anxiety through avoiding.*

> **Second**, *when you repeatedly confront situations that you have avoided because you think that they are dangerous and you find out that nothing bad has happened, you learn that these situations are actually safe and you do not need to avoid them. However, if you continue to avoid, you will continue to believe that these situations are dangerous and you will continue to avoid them. Thus in vivo exposure helps you to better discriminate situations that actually may be dangerous or high risk from those that are actually safe. If you felt okay going to the grocery store alone before, then it is probably OK to do it now.*

> **Third**, *many people with PTSD believe that if they remain in the situation that makes them anxious, their anxiety will remain indefinitely or even get worse and worse. However, if you stay in the situation long enough, you will find that your anxiety will diminish. This process is called habituation. As a result of this process your symptoms will decline.*

Fourth, confronting feared situations and getting over your fears will enhance your self-esteem and make you feel generally more competent, because you will know that you can cope successfully with your problems. You will start doing things that you used to like and that you stopped doing because of your PTSD, and you will begin to enjoy life and expand your activities.

For all these reasons we ask you to systematically confront relatively safe situations that you are now avoiding, beginning with easier ones and progressing toward more difficult situations. Of course we do not suggest that you confront unsafe situations. The goal is not to help you view dangerous situations as safe, but rather to stop avoiding situations that are realistically safe. In order to help you stop avoiding situations and people that were once enjoyable or important, we are going to work together to make a list of situations that you have been avoiding since the trauma. I also want to find out from you how much distress or discomfort these situations will cause you if you confront rather than avoid them.

Using examples of in vivo exposure from real-life situations is extremely helpful to demonstrate how this procedure works and at the same time to demystify the process.

Use one of the following examples to illustrate this point to the client:

Case Example #1: In Vivo Exposure

◾ *Let's talk about an example that illustrates how in vivo exposure works. A little boy was sitting on the beach with his mother when an unexpected, forceful wave from the ocean washed over them. The child got extremely upset and cried that he wanted to go home. The next day when it was time to go to the beach, the little boy began crying and refused to go. He kept saying "No, no. Water come to me." In order to help him overcome his fear of the water, his mother took him for walks on the beach over the next few days. She held his hand and gradually helped him walk closer to the water's edge. By the end of the week the boy was able to walk into the water alone. With patience, practice, encouragement, and gradual exposure, his fear of the water decreased.* ◾

Case Example #2: In Vivo Exposure

■ *A taxicab driver who lived in New York had a fear of driving across bridges. This fear created serious problems with his work, since he was unable to drive people across bridges. Each time he was about to cross a bridge, he pretended that something was wrong with the taxi and called another cab to take his passengers. The taxicab driver, with the help of a therapist, practiced driving over bridges every day. Within a week, he was able to go across the bridge with the therapist following him in another car. By the end of 2 weeks, with repeated practice, he was able to drive over small bridges by himself.* ■

Continue to explain the technique of in vivo exposure to the client:

■ *This was an example to help you understand how systematic confrontation with a feared situation can reduce your level of discomfort. Because you have experienced a traumatic event, you may need more time to confront fears related to your experience. But with time, practice, and courage you will be able to confront the things that now make you afraid.* ■

For clients who have been confronting their feared situations without reduction of anxiety, it may be useful for the therapist to clarify the distinction between occasional, brief exposure and *therapeutic* exposure: deliberate, repeated, prolonged exposure to feared situations. The therapist should explain that only the latter is effective in ameliorating phobia or excessive fear and that together they will take a look at how the client has been trying to face her fears, with the aim of figuring out what is interfering with habituation.

Introduction to SUDS (5 minutes)

Use the following explanation of the SUDS scale before beginning to construct a hierarchy of feared and avoided situations.

In order to find out how much discomfort or anxiety certain situations cause you, we will use a scale that we call the SUDS scale, which stands for Subjective Units of Discomfort. It's a 0 to 100 scale. A

SUDS rating of 100 indicates that you are extremely upset, the most you have ever been in your life, and 0 indicates no discomfort at all, or complete relaxation. Usually when people say they have a SUDS of 100, they may be experiencing physical reactions, such as sweaty palms, palpitations, difficulty breathing, feelings of dizziness, and anxiety. So 100 indicates very extreme fear or anxiety. But because people are different, what makes one person feel 100 SUDS may not be troublesome at all for someone else. This is why we call it a subjective scale. For example, imagine that you and I are standing near a deep pool, and someone pushes us both in the water. If I cannot swim, I will feel a SUDS level of 100 immediately. But if you can swim, or are not afraid of deep water, you may be a 0. Make sense?

Work with the client to identify SUDS anchor points at 0, 50, and 100. To do this, say:

*In order to make this SUDS scale fit you and your particular fears, we will now find out what situations represent different SUDS levels on the scale. So, in what situation that you've been recently have you had a 0 level of discomfort—what makes **you** feel a 0? In what situation have you been a 100—the most distressed, upset, and terrified you've ever been? Now what is a 50 for you? A 50 is a moderate level of distress, halfway between the way you feel when [insert the "0" anchor situation] and [insert the "100" anchor situation].*

It may be useful to have the client also identify anchor points for SUDS levels of 25 and 75. To check whether the client understood the scale, ask the client:

How much discomfort are you feeling now as we are talking? What was your SUDS level when the trauma was over?

Refer to these anchor points when you ask for SUDS ratings until the client becomes familiar with this system. It is helpful to try to establish anchor points that are not directly related to the trauma situation, as the client's fear of these situations may change over the course of therapy. However, for many trauma survivors, the 100 anchor point will be the moment during the trauma that bothers them the most at present; for others, it may be something different. For example:

0 = watching TV in bed, very relaxed

25 = Taking a bus across town

50 = Making a mistake and being asked to meet the boss and explain
the mistake

75 = Getting a phone call from my child's teacher

100 = How I felt during the worse moment of the trauma

> *We are going to be using SUDS ratings to monitor your progress dur-*
> *ing the imaginal and in vivo exposures. We will use this scale during*
> *exposure exercises to monitor change in your anxiety.*

In Vivo Exposure Hierarchy Construction (20 minutes)

Having introduced the client to the rationale for the in vivo exposure
procedures and the SUDS scale, elicit specific examples from her about
situations, people, and places that she avoids because of her trauma.

It is important that the situations are easily accessible for repeated practice, like going to a supermarket or crowded places. Situations that require a 3-hour drive each way are unrealistic for repeated practice. The
situations should also be specific rather than general. For example,
"going into a crowded street" or "going to a supermarket" are not specific enough. It is important to ask the client to designate a specific street
or a specific supermarket, and at a specific time, because different streets
and supermarkets and times of day may be associated with different levels of discomfort. Also, going to the supermarket with a friend may be
less anxiety evoking than going alone.

For some clients, constructing a hierarchy is easily done, and you will
have 15–20 situations fairly quickly. For others, especially those who are
not accustomed to thinking of their behavior in terms of avoidance,
constructing the list will be more challenging. For these clients, you may
not have sufficient time during the session to develop the entire list. It
may be best to concentrate on identifying five situations, of which at
least two are rated in the 40–50 SUDS range, so you can assign them as
homework. Part of the client's homework will be to add more avoided

situations to the list, so that the list will eventually include 15–20 situations. Think of the in vivo hierarchy as a work in progress, and through treatment you and your client may add new situations to the list. Also, the list does not need to be exhaustive, including every situation the client avoids, but merely representative of avoided situations.

There are three types of situations that are commonly avoided by clients with PTSD, and all may need to be considered when constructing the in vivo hierarchy.

1. First are situations that clients perceive as dangerous, not because they are objectively harmful but because the client sees the world as a very dangerous place. The client does not discriminate between truly high-risk situations and relatively low-risk or safe situations. Situations of this type may include walking alone in safe areas after dark, attending a party, going to crowded places, and being in parking lots. This type of situation is avoided because the client believes that she will be harmed or that something really bad will happen if she is in the situation.

2. Second are situations that are reminders of the traumatic event, such as wearing the same or similar clothing, smelling odors or hearing music that were present during the trauma, or watching the news on TV for fear they will hear about a trauma similar to theirs. This type of situation is avoided not because the client perceives them as dangerous but because they trigger memories of the traumatic event and cause distress, fear, shame, or helplessness. These are often objectively quite safe as exposures despite the level of distress or anxiety they arouse.

3. The third type of in vivo exercise is particularly helpful for clients who are depressed or who avoid situations and activities not because they trigger anxiety or distress but because the clients lost interest in them after the trauma. These include things like reengaging in sports, exercise, clubs, hobbies, and friendships; going to church or synagogue or meetings; visiting friends or inviting people to one's home for a meal; and generally doing other activities that the clients used to enjoy but have stopped doing. This type of "behavioral activation" should be added to the in vivo exposure list for clients who are depressed, socially isolated, and/or

inactive, in an effort to help them reconnect to other people and to the world, even if it does not trigger anxiety or other negative emotions.

To construct the in vivo hierarchy, list the avoided situations and activities on the In Vivo Exposure Hierarchy found in appendix B. You may photocopy the form from this book or download it from the Treatments-*ThatWork*™ Web site at www.oup.com/us/ttw. In the column headed "Sess. 2," record the client's anticipated SUDS ratings (i.e., the intensity of anxiety or fear she experiences or imagines she will experience) when confronting each situation. Have the client record the exact same situations on the In Vivo Exposure Hierarchy in her workbook, along with the anticipated SUDS ratings. If the client is not able to come up with avoided situations, use the information already gathered to start the conversation. Explore common areas of avoidance for specific trauma types; for instance, riding in cars for motor vehicle accident survivors or hugs for people who have been assaulted. Use information from the assessment, behavioral observations of the client, or examples from the list provided if the client has difficulty identifying situations. We have included three sample hierarchies for different types of victims and trauma in figures 4.1, 4.2, and 4.3.

List of Typically Avoided Situations for Trauma Survivors

Some typical examples of distressing situations for trauma survivors that usually lead to avoidance are:

1. In cases of assault, being in the presence of unfamiliar men, especially of the same race or physical characteristics as the assailant

2. Someone standing close or approaching suddenly

3. Being touched by someone (especially someone unfamiliar)

4. Engaging in activities similar to the trauma situation (e.g., for motor vehicle accident survivors, driving or riding in a car)

5. Walking down a street or being out in the open

6. Being alone at home (day or night)

7. Going somewhere alone at night

8. Being in a crowded mall or store

9. Talking to strangers

10. Driving a car or being stopped at a stoplight

11. Being in a parking lot

12. Riding in elevators or being in small, confined spaces

13. Reading about a similar event in the newspaper or hearing about it on television

14. Talking with someone about the trauma

15. Watching movies that remind one of a trauma (e.g., combat films, assault scenes)

16. Going to the vicinity of the traumatic event

17. Riding public transportation

18. Hugging and kissing significant others

19. Sexual or physical contact

20. Listening to a song that the client heard during the traumatic event or that was from that same time

21. Watching the news on TV

22. Wearing makeup or looking attractive

23. Going to a movie that involves some violence

24. Enrolling in an exercise class

Safety Considerations When Constructing the In Vivo Exposure Hierarchy

It is important that the situations chosen for in vivo exposure are objectively safe or low risk. The in vivo exposure exercises are selected by the client and the therapist with consideration of safety and relevance of the situations to the client's daily functioning. If the therapist is unfamiliar

Name: _____

Date: _____

Therapist: _____

Item	SUDS (Sess. 2)	SUDS (Sess. 9)	SUDS (Final Sess.)
1. Go out for meal with close friends	25	15	5
2. Go to mall with a friend	30	5	5
3. Go to market with son	30	0	0
4. Go to market alone	35	5	5
5. Go to mall alone	35	10	5
6. Watch someone else handle a knife	45	5	5
7. See a knife outside of kitchen	45	10	0
8. See a movie involving a stabbing	50	15	15
9. Go out to a club with a female friend	50	10	0
10. Go to house of male friend and watch movie	50	25	25
11. See a knife in the bedroom	60	15	5
12. Look at scars on body	70	5	0
13. Go to certain bars with a friend	90	40	30

Anchor points for SUDS scale:

0 – Being in my house watching TV
25 – Being in a public place with a man
50 – Being alone with a man
100 – The way I felt when I realized he was trying to kill me

Figure 4.1

Example of completed In Vivo Exposure Hierarchy for female stabbing survivor.

Name: _____

Date: _____

Therapist: _____

Item	SUDS (Sess. 2)	SUDS (Sess. 9)	SUDS (Final Sess.)
1. See other vets	25	25	0
2. Visit army base	50	25	20
3. Look up war buddies	50	10	5
4 Watch war action movies	75	25	25
5. Call friend and explain why I retired	75	0	
6. Go to beach	75	5	0
7. Be at VA hospital for appointment	80	0	0
8. Wear combat boots	90	0	0
9. Talk about war with wife	90	100	45
10. Go on a cruise	100	0	0
11. Look through old war memorabilia	100	0	10
12. Talk about war experience with other vets	100	25	25

Anchor points for SUDS scale:

0 — Lying in bed, reading, watching TV
25 — Paying bills and being short on money
50 — Arguing with my wife
75 — Losing my job
100 — Being involved in a disaster, violent act

Figure 4.2

Example of completed In Vivo Exposure Hierarchy for male combat veteran.

Name: _____

Date: _____

Therapist: _____

Item	SUDS (Sess. 2)	SUDS (Sess. 9)	SUDS (Final Sess.)
1. Write letter to grandfather (perpetrator)	50	25	
2. Write letter to mother	50	10	
3. Initiate sex with partner	30	5	
4 Lock car doors when parking	40	0	
5. Sleep in bedroom with door unlocked	50	5	
6. Visit mother's family	50	35	20
7. Respond to boyfriend's initiation	60	5	
8. Sleep with bedroom door open	70	5	
9. Walk to town with a friend	70	40	0
10. Sit with back to people	75	15	0
11. Sit in the front of classroom	80	40	30
12. Walk alone to town	85	50	30
13. Visit father's family	85	40	10
13. Talk with mother about abuse	95	20	

Anchor points for SUDS scale:

0 — Sitting at home, doing cross-stitch, watching TV
50 — The time I was followed to my car
100 — The abuse

Figure 4.3

Example of completed In Vivo Exposure Hierarchy for female survivor of childhood sexual abuse.

with the places, activities, or situations that the client avoids, it is important to ask about normative behavior for the client's peer group in that situation. For example, if you are considering whether or not it is safe for a woman to walk outside alone in her neighborhood, ask: "Do other women you know do this? Do women in your neighborhood walk outside alone, and how late do they do this?"

Situations that are objectively dangerous or high risk should not be assigned. For example, the client should not be asked to walk alone in areas where drugs are known to be sold or in a park where ongoing criminal activity is known to take place. Instead, alternate exposures should be designed that include elements that trigger anxiety while preserving safety. For example, the client could walk in a public park with another person or arrange to walk alone in a relatively safe area of the city. If there is doubt about the objective safety of an activity after discussing it with the client, it may be best to forgo that activity.

The following are examples of situations that need safety consideration:

Case Example #1: Safety Considerations

Betty lives in a dangerous inner-city neighborhood. When she leaves her apartment during the evening, she needs to be accompanied by someone. Because of the potential danger involved, the therapist, together with Betty, developed a list of supportive individuals who could accompany her during her in vivo exposure homework.

Case Example #2: Safety Considerations

Veronica was raped in a public parking garage close to her place of employment. Consequently, she avoided going to work because she was afraid of using the only parking garage available to her. In order to help her return to work and use this parking garage, the in vivo exposure assignments included visits to the garage. In order to decrease the probability that Veronica would be revictimized because the garage was located in a high-crime area, it was suggested that when leaving after dark, she should arrange to be escorted by the security guards who worked in the garage.

In Vivo Homework Assignment (5 minutes)

Information for Therapist

In vivo exposure begins with situations that evoke moderate levels of anxiety (e.g., SUDS = 40 or 50) and gradually progresses to the more distressing situations (e.g., SUDS = 100). During the in vivo exposure exercise, the client will be asked to remain in the situation for 30–45 minutes or until her anxiety decreases considerably. Emphasize the goal of remaining in the situation until her SUDS decreases by at least 50%. It is preferable that the client does not feel relief when exiting an exposure. Characteristics of the situations, such as time of day and the people that are present, can be adjusted to achieve the desired level of anxiety during exposure. For example, for Martha, going to the mall with her mother evoked SUDS of 60, while going alone evoked SUDS of 85. So Martha first went to the mall with her mother, and then progressed up her hierarchy to going alone.

A second example involves Brian, a physician, who was attacked by a patient. Brian reported that he experienced 100 SUDS while conducting physical exams of his male patients, but his SUDS ratings decreased to 60 when another person was present during the exams.

It is important to maximize the potential for a successful learning experience early in treatment by carefully selecting the first few in vivo exposure assignments. Therefore, in this session, the first session in which you assign in vivo exposure homework to the client, guide her to select a couple of situations that she has a high likelihood of successfully completing, with some reduction in anxiety. These may be situations that the client has difficulty confronting but can already manage if necessary. Early success increases confidence and motivation to continue by helping the client learn that she *can* benefit from exposure.

Discussion of the client's previous and successful experiences with natural exposure situations can also help instill confidence (e.g., learning to ride a bike, becoming comfortable in the dark, speaking up in groups). By pointing to these examples, the therapist helps the client see that she has already successfully done exposure.

OK, before I assign your in vivo homework let's briefly review the rationale. The goal of in vivo exposure is to enable you to be in situations that remind you of the trauma without experiencing intense anxiety that disrupts your life. This part of the program involves having you confront situations that generate both anxiety and a need to avoid. For it to work, you will have to do a lot of exposure exercises, for a long period of time, each time.

Review the In Vivo Exposure Hierarchy with the client and decide together which situations she will confront for homework. It is best to assign two or more situations for homework rather than one.

Start with situations that were rated between 40 and 50 SUDS. For a client who is particularly avoidant and very anxious about in vivo homework, you may need to start even lower (i.e., 25–30 SUDS range) in order to maximize chance of successful exposure. By the end of treatment, the client should have repeatedly practiced all the situations listed on the hierarchy.

Follow the instructions provided to instruct the client about in vivo exposure. Once the situations for practice have been determined, explain the procedure to the client using the following dialogue:

When you are practicing in the mall, for example, you may initially experience anxiety symptoms, such as your heart beating rapidly, your palms sweating, feeling faint; you may want to leave the situation immediately. But in order to get over the fear it is important that you remain in the situation until your anxiety decreases and you realize that what you were afraid could happen (e.g., being attacked or "falling apart") did not actually happen. Once your anxiety has decreased a good deal or by at least 50%, then you can stop the exposure and resume other activities. However, if you leave the situation when you are very anxious, you are again telling yourself that the situation is dangerous, that anxiety will remain forever, or that something terrible is going to happen to you. And the next time you go into that situation, your level of anxiety will be high again.

Client Name: _Mr. B_   Date: _8/2/05_

1) Situation that you practiced _walking around the army base for a couple of hours_

Date & Time	SUDS			Date & Time	SUDS		
	Pre	Post	Peak		Pre	Post	Peak
1. 8/3/05 4pm	80	75	85	5.			
2. 8/4/05 10am	30	20	60	6.			
3. 8/8/05 3pm	50	50	70	7.			
4. 8/9/05 4pm	40	25	55	8.			

On 8/4/06, I went to base with my wife instead of alone — it was easier that day

2) Situation that you practiced _watching the evening news — hearing about war_

Date & Time	SUDS			Date & Time	SUDS		
	Pre	Post	Peak		Pre	Post	Peak
1. 8/4/05 6pm	50	60	75	5. 8/8/05 6pm	35	35	50
2. 8/5/05 6pm	55	45	60	6. 8/9/05 6pm	40	35	55
3. 8/6/05 6pm	35	50	55	7.			
4. 8/7/05 6pm	40	40	60	8.			

3) Situation that you practiced _attending PTSD group at VA and talking in meeting_

Date & Time	SUDS			Date & Time	SUDS		
	Pre	Post	Peak		Pre	Post	Peak
1. 8/10/05	90	40	90	5.			
2. 8/17/05	80	30	80	6.			
3.				7.			
4.				8.			

Figure 4.4

Example of completed In Vivo Exposure Homework Recording Form for combat veteran.

Client Name: __Ms. S__   Date: __2/15/06__

1) Situation that you practiced __walking dog in the park__

Date & Time	SUDS			Date & Time	SUDS		
	Pre	Post	Peak		Pre	Post	Peak
1. 2/22/06 1pm	60	40	80	5. 2/26/06 2pm	30	30	40
2. 2/23/06 2pm	55	40	60	6. 2/28/06 3pm	30	20	35
3. 2/24/06 6pm	70	50	70	7.			
4. 2/25/06 1pm	40	30	50	8.			

2) Situation that you practiced __going to a movie__

Date & Time	SUDS			Date & Time	SUDS		
	Pre	Post	Peak		Pre	Post	Peak
1. 2/25/06 4pm	50	30	75	5.			
2. 2/28/06 7pm	40	30	55	6.			
3.				7.			
4.				8.			

3) Situation that you practiced __talking to male coworker in the lunchroom__

Date & Time	SUDS			Date & Time	SUDS		
	Pre	Post	Peak		Pre	Post	Peak
1. 2/22/06 12pm	75	75	90	5.			
2. 2/24/06 12pm	75	60	80	6.			
3. 2/27/06 10am	60	45	60	7.			
4.				8.			

Note — the last time I did this, I sat and talked to a guy for over 1 hour, and definitely felt my nervousness get better, but was still worried that he'd ask me out or something.

Figure 4.5

Example of completed In Vivo Exposure Homework Recording Form for rape survivor.

On the other hand, if you stay in the situation and you realize that you are not really in danger, your anxiety will decrease, and eventually you will be able to enter the situation without fear. The more frequently you practice each situation on your list, the faster you will reach the point where you will stop being anxious in those situations. As a result you will feel less of an urge to avoid situations and people that are now distressing for you.

Show the client how to record her SUDS during exposure homework on the In Vivo Exposure Homework Recording Form found in the workbook. We have included two sample forms in figures 4.4 and 4.5. Explain that she should rate her SUDS level before and after the exposure, as well as the peak, or highest, SUDS level.

Homework (10 minutes)

✎ Instruct client to continue daily breathing practice.

✎ Ask client to read about the common reactions to trauma in the workbook several times a week; client should share this with significant others.

✎ Ask client to review the In Vivo Exposure Hierarchy at home and add additional situations.

✎ Client should also review the Model for Gradual In Vivo Exposure in the workbook.

✎ Instruct client to begin in vivo assignments.

✎ Ask client to listen to audiotape of entire session once.

Chapter 5   *Session 3*

(Corresponds to chapter 5 of the workbook)

Materials Needed

- Two audiotapes to record session
- Therapist Imaginal Exposure Recording Form
- Imaginal Exposure Homework Recording Form
- In Vivo Exposure Homework Recording Form

Session Outline

- Review homework (10–15 minutes)
- Present agenda for session (3 minutes)
- Present rationale for imaginal exposure (10–15 minutes)
- Conduct imaginal exposure (45–60 minutes)
- Process imaginal exposure (15–20 minutes)
- Assign homework (5 minutes)

Homework Review (10–15 minutes)

Review the preceding week's homework with the client. You should spend a good amount of time reviewing the in vivo exposure homework, looking at the In Vivo Exposure Homework Recording Form with the client, and scanning for patterns of change in SUDS or evidence of habituation. Ask the client what he learned from doing these exposures and how helpful he found them. Offer ample praise for the client's efforts. Ask him how often he used the breathing retraining and read the Common Reactions to Trauma information in the workbook, and how useful these were during the last week. Discuss his reactions to listening to the audiotape of the session.

If the client did not complete the homework, ask about the reasons and indicate that more discussion about how the homework can be accomplished will be conducted later during homework assignment.

Set Agenda (3 minutes)

Explain to the client the following plan for the session:

Last session we discussed why we ask you to confront situations that cause you to feel anxious or upset in this program. Today we're going to spend part of the session discussing in detail how confronting your trauma memories will help you overcome your PTSD symptoms. Then I'm going to ask you to revisit and recount the trauma for about 45–60 minutes. Afterward, we'll spend some time processing this experience together and discussing your thoughts and feelings about the trauma. At the end of the session we'll leave some time to discuss the in vivo and imaginal exposure exercises you will do for your homework.

Information for Therapist

Imaginal exposure, or revisiting the trauma memory in imagery, is a procedure in which the client is asked to visualize and emotionally connect with the traumatic event while recounting the experience aloud, in the present tense. It is not a conversation between you and the client. The standard procedure is designed to:

- Enhance the client's ability to access all of the salient aspects of the trauma memory: events, thoughts, emotions, and sensory experiences

- Promote emotional engagement with the trauma memory

- Invite narration of the memory in the client's own words with minimal direction and prompting by the therapist

Allow the client to approach the trauma memory gradually the first time the client revisits and recounts the trauma memory. In general, do not be too directive when the client describes the trauma experience. It is important that the client feel in control of the process of remembering the trauma and the feelings associated with it. Therefore, give the client permission to approach the memories at his own pace, and provide a calm and supportive presence.

Clients are sometimes reluctant to engage fully with the emotional aspects of recounting the trauma memory. It may be helpful for you to remind the client that he can confront the feared images gradually. For example, during the first and second sessions of imaginal revisiting (exposure) of the trauma memory, the client should be allowed to determine the level of detail with which he recounts the narrative of his trauma. In subsequent imaginal exposures, he should be encouraged to describe the event in more detail by probing for the emotional, cognitive, and physiological reactions that occurred during the trauma.

Prolonged or Multiple Incident Traumas

For clients with a prolonged trauma (e.g., a period of torture, several days of captivity) or multiple incident traumas (e.g., repeated assaults, recurring childhood sexual abuse, multiple incidents of combat), you will need to establish which of the traumatic memories will be the focus of imaginal exposure. Typically, these are the memories that are the most intrusive and distressing at the present time. Choosing a memory to focus on should begin during session 1 when you ask about trauma history and continue in session 3 prior to beginning imaginal exposure. If you are unsure which memory to choose, ask the client which memory is haunting him the most through intrusive, distressing thoughts, flashbacks, or nightmares.

In most cases, successful processing of the most disturbing memory will generalize to less distressing memories so that they too will become less distressing. However, if the client is extremely anxious and uncertain whether he can manage the "worst" memory, have him first choose a trauma memory that he feels he can manage and then move up to the most distressing memory after the first memory ceases to elicit high anxiety. Sometimes, even after processing the most distressing memory, another traumatic experience continues to trigger high levels of distress. In this case proceed to using imaginal exposure with that memory after the first memory is much less distressing. We include more detail on conducting imaginal exposure later in the chapter.

Processing

After the imaginal revisiting of the trauma memory you will process the experience with the client for approximately 15–20 minutes. In brief, processing involves encouraging the client to talk about his reactions to revisiting the trauma memory and discussing feelings and thoughts that he may have about the trauma or its meaning in his life. The process of imaginal recounting of the trauma memory creates powerful opportunities for learning. It is common for clients to emerge from imaginal (and in vivo) exposure with new awareness or insights. Asking the client to describe and expand on these insights makes them more explicit, and he often begins to reevaluate and modify unrealistic views or expectations. Guidelines for how to facilitate this processing are provided.

It is important that the client not leave the session in great distress or with high anxiety. Treatment sessions should be planned so that there will be sufficient time at the end of the session to help the client alleviate his distress level. In cases in which the client remains very distressed, breathing retraining after the imaginal exposure may be helpful. It is also helpful to tell the client that he may feel temporarily more upset after some exposure sessions, especially the early ones, and relief after others. Finally, it may be helpful to tell the client that anxiety and distress during imaginal recounting of the trauma memory reflect the beginning of emotional processing of the distressing memories, i.e., the beginning of healing from the trauma. If the client is very apprehensive about his reaction to the early sessions of imaginal exposure, it is fine if he brings a supportive person with him to wait and drive home with him after the session.

Rationale for Imaginal Exposure (15 minutes)

Presentation to Client

Present the client with the following rationale for prolonged imaginal exposure:

> *Today we are going to spend most of the session helping you revisit the memory of your [name the actual trauma or use client's language for the traumatic incident, e.g., the car accident]. It is not easy to understand and make sense of traumatic experiences. The trauma was a very frightening and distressing experience, so it is natural that you try to push away or avoid the painful memories. You may tell yourself, "Don't think about it; time heals all wounds," or "I just have to forget about it." Other people often advise you to use these same tactics. Also, your friends, family, and partner may feel uncomfortable hearing about the trauma, and this may influence you not to talk about it. But, as you have already discovered, no matter how hard you try to push away thoughts about the trauma, the memory comes back to haunt you through distressing thoughts and feelings, nightmares, and flashbacks. These reexperiencing symptoms are a sign that the trauma is still "unfinished business."*

Make the point that it is difficult, if not impossible, to successfully push powerful images and memories out of your mind and that focusing on the images and memories instead can be helpful.

> *Let me demonstrate to you how trying hard to push a thought out of your mind actually can make this thought stronger. For the next 10 seconds, I want you to think about anything that comes into your mind, EXCEPT one thing. Whatever you do, DO NOT think about a pink elephant floating above my head. [Wait several seconds.] What are you thinking about now? I bet you are thinking about a pink elephant.*

Below we provide several metaphors that help demonstrate to the client why it is particularly difficult, yet important, to process the traumatic memory. You do not need to use all of them. Instead, choose the one that makes most sense to you.

In order to explain to you why it is so important to process the trau-
matic memory, I want to give you an example:

1. Suppose you have eaten a very large and heavy meal (or spoiled
food) and now you have symptoms such as stomachache, nausea, etc.
These symptoms will stay until you have digested the food. After the
food has been digested you will feel great relief. Flashbacks, night-
mares, and troublesome thoughts continue to occur because you have
not digested the traumatic memory. Today you are going to start di-
gesting or processing your heavy memories so that they will stop inter-
fering with your daily life.

Another way to explain why it is so difficult to digest and process a traumatic memory is by the following example:

2. Imagine that your memory is like a very elaborate file cabinet. Past
experiences are each filed into a proper drawer. In this way you organ-
ize your experiences and make sense of them. For example, you have a
file for restaurant experiences. Every time you go to eat in a restaurant,
you open the restaurant file and you know what will happen. This is
the way in which you remember how to behave in a restaurant and
what to expect. But traumatic events do not have a file. This is be-
cause, unlike the restaurant experience where you know exactly what
will happen (you will be seated, given a menu, you will choose your
food, get a check, and pay), traumas are unpredictable. Even if you
have had several traffic accidents in which you were not injured, you
never know how the next accident will end. In this way each trauma
is unique and therefore needs much more effort to process. Part of
recovering from a traumatic experience is being able to organize the
traumatic memory, to file it in long-term memory so you can move on
with the business of your life.

The following example is especially helpful for the client who comments
that he thinks about the trauma all the time and questions the utility of
repeated revisiting of the traumatic event:

Imagine that your traumatic event is recorded in your brain like a
book, with paragraphs, pages, and sections. Like all books, your trau-
matic event book is a story with a beginning, middle, and end. Be-
cause you try to avoid thinking about your trauma, you have not read

the book from the beginning to the end since the trauma occurred.
Whenever you have a flashback, the book is opened at the paragraph
where the flashback is written and opening the book is painful and
distressing. So you say to yourself, "I don't like this book," and you try
hard to close it. The same thing happens when you have the next
flashback or thought about your trauma. And this is why you have not
read what is written in the book. In imaginal exposure, we will read
the book together from the beginning to the end. This will give you an
opportunity to view the traumatic event and its meaning from your
perspective today, rather than from the perspective of the past when
the trauma happened and you felt terrified.

After explaining to your client why it is especially difficult to process and
digest a traumatic memory, present the rationale for how repeated imaginal exposure facilitates the processing of this memory:

Let's discuss now how repeatedly revisiting and recounting the memory
that distresses you so much will help you process it and overcome your
PTSD symptoms.

First, repeatedly retelling your memory will help you organize the
memory and get new perspective about what happened during and
after the trauma. Second, repeated revisiting of the trauma will help
you differentiate between "remembering" your traumatic event and
"being retraumatized." Many people with PTSD feel that when they
think or talk about their trauma it feels as if it is happening again.
Do you sometimes feel this way?

Briefly discuss the client's experience.

This confusion between remembering and being retraumatized ex-
plains why people with PTSD are so anxious and distressed when they
think about the trauma. Fear is an emotion we have when we feel im-
minent danger. However, remembering a trauma that occurred 2 or 3
years ago is not dangerous. But if, when remembering, you feel as if
you are traumatized again, it makes sense that you will be very anx-
ious. Revisiting the traumatic memory again and again will help you
strengthen the differentiation between the present (remembering) and
the past (being traumatized), and as a result, remembering the trauma
will cease to elicit distress and anxiety. Third, repeated imaginal expo-

sure to your trauma memory for an extended period of time will lower anxiety. We call this habituation. When this happens you learn that anxiety does not last "forever," even if you stay in the memory rather than pushing it away. Fourth, repeatedly revisiting your memory in imagination promotes differentiation between the traumatic event and similar events and thereby will decrease the generalization of fear from your specific trauma to similar but safe situations. For example, a rape victim may generalize her fear of the assailant to men that remind her of the assailant. Repeatedly imaging the particular assailant (e.g., his blue eyes) will help differentiate that man from all other men, thus reducing the fear of men in general. [Important note: Use an example from the client's own trauma to demonstrate how imaginal exposure decreases generalization.]

Fifth, repeatedly recounting your memory enhances your sense of self-control and personal competence. You feel progressively better about yourself as you stop avoiding and master your fears. You will be able to remember the trauma when you want to and put it aside when you don't want to think about it. And you will be in control of your traumatic memory instead of it controlling you, what you do and what you don't do.

Summarize for the client:

So the goal of imaginal revisiting and recounting your trauma is to enable you to have thoughts about the trauma, talk about it, or see triggers associated with it without experiencing the intense anxiety that now disrupts your life. This part of the program involves having you confront trauma-related memories that generate both anxiety and an urge to avoid. For it to work, we'll do it repeatedly, for an extended period each time.

Before we begin, do you have any questions about anything that I have said?

In summary, the rationale for imaginal exposure includes the following five points:

1. Processing and organizing the memory

2. Promoting differentiation between "remembering" the traumatic event and "being retraumatized"

3. Promoting habituation

4. Promoting differentiation between the traumatic event and similar events

5. Increased mastery and sense of control

Conducting Imaginal Exposure (45–60 minutes)

Presentation to Client

Explain the imaginal exposure procedure to the client. It is typical for a client to have some trepidation. Reassure him and continue to present the following explanation.

I'm going to ask you to recall the memories of the trauma. It's best to start the revisiting at a point in the memory that is a little bit before the trauma actually occurred, so that you have a chance to enter the image and get connected to it. So you may want to begin your story at a point that is at least several minutes before the situation got bad or frightening. You will then go on through the story of the trauma, up until the danger is over or you are out of the situation. [Important note: select specific beginning and ending points with the client before progressing further.]

It is best for you to close your eyes while you do this so you won't be distracted. I will ask you to recall these painful memories as vividly as possible and to picture them in your mind's eye. We call this revisiting the trauma memory. What I would like you to do is describe the experience in the present tense, as if it were happening now, right here. I'd like you to recount aloud what happened during the trauma in as much detail as you can manage today. We will work on this together. If you start to feel uncomfortable and want to run away or avoid it by leaving the image, I will help you to stay with it. From time to time, while you are revisiting the trauma, I will ask you for your anxiety level on the 0 to 100 SUDS scale. Please just try to answer quickly with the first number that comes to mind to describe how you feel here today, sitting in this chair, and don't leave the image. Because it is im-

portant that we stay in the imaginal exposure for a lengthy period of time, when you finish recounting the trauma, I'll ask you to start all over again, without pause. We may do this several times within today's session; how many times depends on how long it takes you to go through the memory. It's important that you do not push the memories away, even if they are painful. Remember, memories are not dangerous, even if they feel bad. I will not say much in response to you until your imaginal exposure is done, but we'll have time afterward to talk about your experience with it. Do you have any questions before we start?

Answer any questions the client has, but begin the imaginal exposure as soon as possible, since the client may be increasingly anxious until he begins. Have the client recount the traumatic memory for 45–60 minutes without interruption. When he ends one recounting, tell him, "You're doing great. Now I want you to go back to the beginning. So you're walking down the street. Tell me what's happening now," and let the client take over the recounting his memory.

Important: Just before beginning the imaginal exposure, switch from the session audiotape to a new audiotape, in order for the client to have the recounting on a separate tape for use at home. This prevents the client from having to search for the narration of the trauma each time he listens to the tape at home. When the recounting ends, switch back again to the session tape to record the processing and the homework instructions. Thus, from session 3 until the session before the final session, you will have two tapes in each session. One will include the beginning of the session and the end of the session, and the other will be devoted to the client's recounting of the traumatic memory.

Use the Therapist Imaginal Exposure Recording Form provided to record the client's SUDS ratings every 5 minutes and to make notes about things the client says or does that seem important to discuss later. You may photocopy the form from this book or download multiple copies from the Treatments *That Work*™ Web site at www.oup.com/us /ttw. After about 45–60 minutes of imaginal exposure, terminate the exercise by asking the client to open his eyes and end the imaginal experience: "OK, let's stop here. Great job—now let's talk about how this was for you."

Therapist Imaginal Exposure Recording Form

Name of Client: _____ Therapist: _____

Date: _____ Exposure #: _____ Session #: _____

Description of exposure in imagination: _____

_____

_____

Start time	SUDS	Notes
Beginning	_____	_____
5 minutes	_____	_____
10 minutes	_____	_____
15 minutes	_____	_____
20 minutes	_____	_____
25 minutes	_____	_____
30 minutes	_____	_____
35 minutes	_____	_____
40 minutes	_____	_____
45 minutes	_____	_____
50 minutes	_____	_____
55 minutes	_____	_____
60 minutes	_____	_____

Therapeutic Comments During Imaginal Exposure

Although it is important to not engage the client in conversation during his imaginal exposure, it is helpful to let him know that you are there by offering brief but encouraging comments once in awhile. The following statements are examples of supportive comments that may be helpful to the client during the exposure:

1. You are doing fine, stay with the image.

2. You're doing very well. Hang in there.

3. Great job, stay with your feelings.

4. Remember, memories are not dangerous like the trauma was.

5. I know this is difficult. You are doing a good job.

6. Stay with the image, you are safe here.

How to Help the Client Process the Traumatic Memory During Imaginal Exposure

As PE progresses, you will begin to probe for the thoughts, feelings, and physical reactions the client experienced during the traumatic event by asking brief, specific questions while he is recounting the trauma. Below is a list of these kinds of probe questions that you can ask the client in order to facilitate confrontation with fear-evoking cues during imaginal exposure:

■ What are you feeling?

■ What are you thinking?

■ What do you smell?

■ What does it look like?

■ What is your body feeling?

■ Where do you feel that in your body?

Note: If the client spontaneously includes this information in his narration of the traumatic event, you do not need to ask these questions.

As treatment progresses, you will also begin to identify the parts of the narrative that are the most anxiety producing or distressing for the client. We refer to these memories as "hot spots," and these portions of the memory will be recounted in a repetitive fashion (as many as 6–12 times) during a single session. We will describe how to process them in the next chapter.

During the last sessions, for most clients, you should expect SUDS ratings during imaginal recounting of the trauma to range from 20–30 and finally from 10–20. Other clients may continue to rate their SUDS as moderately high throughout treatment. In such cases, you may need to pay more attention to other indicators of improvement (i.e., a decrease in PTSD and depression symptoms, or much less distress than early in treatment). In these cases you may want to discuss the discrepancy between the high SUDS and the other indicators of distress and recalibrate the SUDs ratings if needed. For example, if the client provides SUDS levels of 70–80 during session 9 while his PTSD symptoms have decreased substantially, you might want to remind him that 80 was the rating he had assigned to walking alone in a crowed mall. Then ask him if he now feels the same distress during imaginal exposure as he felt in the beginning of treatment going to crowded places.

Processing the Imaginal Exposure (15–20 minutes)

Imaginal revisiting and recounting of a trauma memory is distressing and challenging, especially in the early sessions of therapy. Therefore, it is important to begin processing the client's exposure by acknowledging his courage in facing and recounting this painful memory and by offering positive comments or praise for what he accomplished. For example: "OK, let's stop here, and open your eyes. you did a great job. Good for you," or "You hung in there really well even though it was pretty distressing to do this; that took a lot of courage," or "You did a great job with that; I know it is really hard to do." For clients who end imaginal exposure feeling very distressed and/or are crying, your first goal is to help them to calm and return to a less distressed state. In doing so, it may be helpful to guide these clients in a few minutes of slow, paced breathing. In general, the amount of support you offer should be tailored to the client's needs and emotional state.

After providing positive feedback (and support if needed), move to processing the recounting experience with the client. Ask him to describe his thoughts and feelings about the imaginal exposure with general, open-ended questions. For example: "How was that for you?" or "What was that like for you?" or "How did that feel?" Allow him to respond as fully as he can or wants to. Processing (throughout the course of therapy) should be focused on encouraging the client to share his perceptions and feelings about the experience of revisiting the trauma and helping him to articulate his thoughts about the trauma and the meaning it has had in his life. During the discussion, look for opportunities to normalize the client's feelings, thoughts, and behavior in the context of trauma and PTSD, and help the client understand and accept his reactions and symptoms.

During the processing, help the client recognize patterns of habituation of distress that occur within or between sessions. Ask, "What did you notice about your anxiety?" If the client's anxiety decreased during the imaginal revisiting, you can make comments such as: "You see, as we have discussed, your anxiety decreases if you just continue to hang in there and stay with the memory," or "I want you to notice that you are much less anxious than you were in the beginning of this session; how do you think this happened?" or (in subsequent sessions): "I can see that you had much less anxiety today than the last time you confronted this distressing memory, and your SUDS levels were lower. So, the more you confront this memory, the less anxious and distressed you are feeling" or "Does it feel as bad as it used to feel?"

If the client's anxiety has *not* decreased during the imaginal exposure, as is often the case in the first few sessions, normalize the lack of habituation and give positive feedback: "You were feeling quite anxious today throughout the imaginal exposure. But despite this, you hung in there, stayed in touch with your feelings and did a great job recounting the memory. You were not sure that you would be able to do this. Good for you!" and "Many times anxiety does not go down during the revisiting of the trauma in the first sessions. But we know from our studies and experience that habituation within the sessions does not predict outcome. We just need to keep working on it," or "Great job! I know that you did not feel less distressed at the end of the exposure this time, and your SUDS level stayed high. But you accomplished an important aspect of our work together: you fully accessed this memory and were really engaged with the feelings and thoughts that are part of the memory. That is a crucial step in processing the trauma."

Clients will often spontaneously express thoughts and feelings during the processing that reflect negative, unhelpful, inaccurate, or unrealistic beliefs. For example, a client who was raped by her boyfriend and his friends said: "If only I let them know how much I did not want to have sex with them, they would have stopped." The accuracy of this statement needs to be explored with the patient with questions like, "What makes you think that they didn't know you did not want to be raped?"

Alternatively the client might make a statement that reflects an emerging shift in perspective or view that seems *more* realistic and appropriate. For example, after listening to her narrative of the rape several times in the sessions and at home, the above client said: "I didn't realize how much I fought them. Of course they knew that I did not want to have sex with them." Follow up on such a statement by encouraging the client to talk more about the new insight: "Tell me more about that," or "That seems really important; what do you think now about your behavior during the rape?" Always help the client elaborate on these important shifts in perspective by asking questions; refrain from *telling* her how she *should* think or feel.

Other statements that are important to address during processing are the client's expressions of unrealistic or excessively negative views of himself, other people, the world, and his ability to cope with the trauma and its aftermath. Explore these "themes" that emerge during exposure. As discussed in detail in the first chapter, these negative cognitions underlie chronic PTSD, and the aim of emotional processing is to incorporate new information that will correct the unrealistic, pathological aspects of the trauma memory. This is achieved through imaginal and in vivo exposure as the client realizes that the world is not always dangerous and that she is capable of coping successfully with the distressing memories and situations. During processing you should facilitate the verbal elaboration of these realizations.

For example, if after imaginal revisiting of the trauma, a client berates herself for not having anticipated the rape and not having "known" that her date was the kind of person who would rape her, you might ask: "I notice that you blame yourself for not knowing that the assault was coming. How do you think you might have anticipated the rape?" or "How does it help you to blame yourself for not foreseeing this assault? How does it hurt you?" or "Do you remember back in session 1 when we talked about what maintains PTSD symptoms over time? One of those important factors was the presence of trauma-related beliefs about oneself or others that are unhelpful or negative. Do you think that any of those kinds of beliefs are present here?"

To summarize, in the processing of imaginal exposure, you should:

- Begin by providing positive feedback and acknowledgment of the client's courage and ability to confront these painful memories.

- Provide support and calming when needed.

- Ask the client to express her thoughts and feelings about the foregoing imaginal revisiting of this traumatic experience.

- Normalize and help her understand her reactions and behaviors in the trauma and its aftermath.

- Comment on habituation that you observe within or across sessions (or lack thereof, as described above).

- After the client has described her thoughts and feelings about the recounting of the memory, you may share your own observations of her imaginal exposure; ask questions about those aspects of the revisiting or the client's emotional responses that seemed particularly important or meaningful to you.

- As therapy progresses and you become aware of the thoughts or beliefs the client holds that may be contributing to the maintenance of her PTSD, begin to focus discussion on these areas during the processing after the imaginal exposure.

- Try to stimulate her thinking with open-ended questions; do not tell the client how she *should* view the trauma or feel about it or how you view it.

Questions that may be useful during processing, especially in later treatment sessions:

- When did you start viewing it this way?

- How do you feel when you think of it in this way?

- What would you tell your daughter/sister/friend if she were thinking this way?

Much of the distress of clients with chronic PTSD may come from perspectives on the trauma that they developed after the trauma occurred, rather than from the particular thoughts that went through their minds at the time the event was happening. To identify these posttrauma thoughts, it is useful to ask clients questions such as:

- What does it mean to you that this happened?

- What does it say about you?

Similar questions can also be asked about the client's appraisal of his PTSD symptoms:

- Why do you think you currently have PTSD?

- What do you think the symptoms say about you?

- How does that fit with what you've learned about common reactions to trauma?

- How does it make you feel to think of yourself in this manner?

Problems the Therapist May Encounter During Imaginal Exposure

Some clients have difficulty expressing their feelings. Some say they are afraid to cry, because they imagine they may never stop. In order to maintain control, the client may engage in avoidance behavior during imagery. For example, he may become quiet and may avoid visualizing extremely upsetting memories, such as the image of an oncoming car just before the crash, an assailant's face, or being threatened with a weapon. On the other hand, some (although few) clients become very involved in the imagery, to the point where they begin to feel overwhelmed or out of control. For these clients, it is helpful to remind them verbally that they are safe in the therapy room with you and that what they are reliving is a memory and is not happening now. In chapter 8 we will discuss ways to modify procedures in order to overcome these problems.

Case Example: Getting Started With Imaginal Exposure

■ *The following case example is provided to demonstrate how to help the client handle his discomfort about starting the imaginal exposure scene.* ■

T: Do you have any questions before we begin?

C: No.

T: You are looking a little apprehensive. How are you feeling?

C: I am feeling very scared. I haven't told this story to anyone except the police.

Client Name: Mr. B   Date: 9/8/05

Instructions: Please record your SUDS ratings on a 0–100 scale (where 0 = no discomfort and 100 = maximal discomfort, anxiety, and panic) before and after you listen to the audiotape of the imaginal exposure.

Tape #: 7 (fourth exposure — hot spots)

DATE & TIME	3/2/06 7pm	3/3/06 5pm	3/4/06 4pm	3/5/06 10am
SUDS Pre	50	50	40	30
SUDS Post	40	30	35	30
Peak SUDS	50	55	40	50

DATE & TIME	3/7/06 7pm	3/8/06 6pm		
SUDS Pre	30	30		
SUDS Post	20	20		
Peak SUDS	50	35		

Figure 5.1

Example of completed Imaginal Exposure Homework Recording Form for combat veteran.

T: I imagine the thought of doing this is very frightening. In fact, we even have a word for this: it is called anticipatory anxiety. Remember how I have talked about habituation? Eventually, imagining the trauma and talking about it will become easier for you. However, the way we get to that point is through repeated practice. In the beginning, revisiting the trauma may be very anxiety producing and, in fact, you may even feel worse before you feel better. This is a signal that you are beginning to process or digest the trauma. I want you to know that I will be here to help you throughout the process. It is important for you to realize that this type of treatment has helped many survivors of trauma and that it will become easier with time. So, let's not delay any further. I want you to go back in your mind's eye to [the place and time of the trauma] and tell me what is happening now.

Client Name: Ms. S   Date: 3/1/06

Instructions: Please record your SUDS ratings on a 0–100 scale (where 0 = no discomfort and 100 = maximal discomfort, anxiety, and panic) before and after you listen to the audiotape of the imaginal exposure.

Tape #: 1 (first exposure)

DATE & TIME	3/2/06 7pm	3/3/06 5pm	3/4/06 4pm	3/5/06 10am
SUDS Pre	80	80	70	40
SUDS Post	70	70	50	60
Peak SUDS	90	80	75	65

DATE & TIME	3/7/06 7pm	3/8/06 6pm		
SUDS Pre	50	40		
SUDS Post	40	30		
Peak SUDS	60	40		

Figure 5.2

Example of completed Imaginal Exposure Homework Recording Form for rape survivor.

Homework (5 minutes)

✎ Instruct the client to listen to the audiotape of imaginal exposure once a day. Tell him that he should choose a time in which he will not be interrupted, and he should listen to the tape of the recounting from beginning to end, without turning it off. He should sit down and listen to the tape with eyes closed and visualizing what he is hearing throughout the tape. Explain to him that the goal is to try to emotionally engage with the feelings he has while listening to the exposure tape at home. If the client is not alone at home, ask him to listen to the tape using headphones in order to preserve his privacy. Caution him, however, to not listen to the tape just before bedtime in order to prevent sleep disturbance or nightmares. Also ask the client not to let others listen to the tape.

✎ Ask the client to record his SUDS levels while listening to the imaginal exposure using the Imaginal Exposure Homework Recording Form in the workbook (see figures 5.1 and 5.2 for sample completed forms).

✎ Help the client choose which in vivo exposure exercises he will do for the coming week. The client should continue with in vivo exposure exercises daily, repeating each exercise until habituation occurs, and then working up the hierarchy with progressively higher SUDS levels.

✎ Instruct the client to listen to the audiotape of the session one time.

✎ Ask the client to come early to the next session to complete self-report forms.

Chapter 6 | *Intermediate Sessions*

(Corresponds to chapter 7 of the workbook)

Materials Needed

- Two audiotapes to record session and imaginal exposure separately

- Therapist Imaginal Exposure Recording Form

- Imaginal Exposure Homework Recording Form

- In Vivo Exposure Homework Recording Form

- Self-report forms for measuring PTSD and depression to be administered every other session (e.g., sessions 4, 6, 8, 10)

Session Outline

- Review homework (10 minutes)

- Present agenda for session (3 minutes)

- Conduct 30–45 minutes of imaginal exposure

- In sessions 5–9 (or close to final session), focus on "hot spots" progressively more as therapy advances. Return to recounting of entire memory when anxiety associated with hot spots has sufficiently reduced, but make sure to do so by final session.

- Process imaginal exposure (15–20 minutes)

- Discuss in vivo exposure (10–15 minutes)

- Assign homework (5 minutes)

Homework Review (10 minutes)

Inspect the client's SUDS ratings of the imaginal and in vivo exposure homework exercises. Discuss changes in SUDS ratings; comment on habituation as it occurs. Inquire about her reactions to listening to the tape of the trauma recounting and the tape of the entire session. Ask questions about what the client learned from her imaginal and in vivo exposure homework. Offer her praise and encouragement.

Note: It is often more efficient to save an in-depth discussion of in vivo homework until the relevant part of the session (e.g., reviewing in vivo homework just before discussing the next in vivo assignments). If you choose to do this, briefly inspect the client's homework rating forms at the beginning of the session, offer praise and positive feedback, and tell her you will discuss it in more detail after today's imaginal exposure.

Every other session (e.g., in sessions 4, 6, 8, and 10), use self-report scales (e.g., the Posttraumatic Stress Disorder Self Report [PDS] and the Beck Depression Inventory [BDI]) to assess the client's PTSD and mood symptoms of the last week. Review these briefly with the client at the beginning of the session. It can be helpful to comment on changes in symptoms as treatment progresses.

Set Agenda (3 minutes)

Offer the client the following agenda for the session:

Today we are going to spend about 30 to 45 minutes of the session recounting your trauma memory. After discussing that experience, we'll spend the remainder of the session planning and talking in detail about this week's in vivo exposures.

Imaginal Exposure (30–45 minutes)

Presentation to Client

Today we will again spend some time revisiting the memory of your [name trauma]. I would like to ask you to slow down during the recounting of your trauma and focus in more detail on what you are

seeing, hearing, and feeling. Again, I will ask you to give me your
SUDS ratings every 5 minutes. When I ask you for your SUDS, I'd
like you to just call out your rating as quickly as possible and don't
leave the image. Just like last time, I'd like you to close your eyes and
to vividly imagine what happened at the time of the [name trauma].
Use the present tense, as if it were occurring now, and include what
happened, and what you were feeling and thinking as you went
through this experience.

At session 5 and subsequent sessions, add: *At this point in our work,*
you should be including all details. If it is in your memory, please say
it out loud. Don't worry about what it sounds like.

Continue imaginal exposure for 30–45 minutes without interruption. The length of time spent recounting the trauma (or number of repetitions) will often depend on how long clients take to go through their narratives and on their patterns of SUDS levels. In general, try to have the client repeat the narrative until distress levels decrease. Even if such habituation does not occur within a session, the recounting of the trauma memory should be terminated early enough that sufficient time remains to process the experience with the client. During processing and homework assignment, the client's distress will decrease.

As the therapy progresses (starting about session 5), you will focus on "hot spots." The hot spots procedure is described in the next section.

Sometimes clients struggle with recounting a memory or expressing their emotions during the imaginal exposure. If a client has particular difficulty with a specific part of the memory, it may help for you to discuss with the client, prior to the exposure, his or her reluctance to engage with or express feelings about the memory. For example, a therapist remarked to one client who had difficulty expressing strong emotions:

"The last two times that you recounted the memory of your trauma, I noticed that you seemed to have difficulty letting go of your feelings. I want to remind you that you are safe here and that an important part of revisiting trauma memories is the connection to the feelings that are associated with them. Is there anything that I can do to help you with this process? Do you have any ideas about why it is difficult for you to fully express your feelings in here?"

Clients who have difficulty accessing or expressing trauma-related feelings are sometimes "under-engaged." In chapter 8 we describe ways to help these clients to increase emotional engagement through modification of the imaginal exposure procedures. Less commonly, clients may be over-engaged in revisiting the trauma, and the therapist must help them to reduce emotional engagement. These procedures are also described in chapter 8.

Hot Spots Procedure

Beginning at session 5 or 6, emotional processing of the trauma memories can be made more efficient by having the client focus primarily or exclusively on the most *currently* distressing parts of the trauma, which we term the "hot spots." The hot spots procedure should be introduced after two to three sessions of imaginal exposure have been conducted and habituation to the relatively less-distressing parts of the memory has begun to occur.

In the session in which you introduce the hot spots procedure, prior to beginning to recount the trauma memory, explain to the client:

> *Up to this point, each time you have revisited the trauma, you have described the entire memory of your [name trauma]. And you have been making great progress and have been experiencing the decrease in anxiety that we expect to see. Today we are going to do the imaginal exposure a little differently. When someone starts getting the benefit that you are having, we begin using a different procedure that helps to emotionally process the most difficult moments. In a minute I will ask you to tell me, based on your last exposure here and on your listening to the imaginal exposure tape last week, what the most distressing or upsetting parts of this memory are for you now. And then today, rather than going through the entire memory from beginning to end, I will ask you to focus the revisiting and recounting on each of these "hot spots," one at a time. We will pick one to begin with and you will repeat that one part of the memory over and over just by itself, focusing in closely and describing what happened in great detail, as if in slow motion, including what you felt, saw, heard, and thought. We will repeat it as many times as necessary to "wear it out" or bring*

about a big decease in your SUDS level. When that part seems to have
been sufficiently processed, we will move to the next one. Any ques-
tions?

Identify the hot spots on the basis of the client's self-report of the currently most distressing moments of the traumatic event and record them
on the therapist form. If the client does not identify a part of the memory that in your perception is likely a hot spot (e.g., the part where the
client always gives high SUDS ratings or avoids that part somewhat during the exposure), ask him or her whether that part is a hot spot as well.

Help the client select a hot spot to begin the exposure. This should be
one of the most distressing parts, if not the most distressing part, of the
trauma.

Focus on the client's hot spots during the imaginal exposure until each
has been sufficiently processed, as reflected by diminished SUDS levels
and the client's behavior (e.g., body movement, facial expression). This
may take several sessions, depending on the number of hot spots, the
client's pace, and the amount of time he or she spends listening to exposure tapes as homework. Sometimes a client gives low SUDS ratings
and/or appears minimally distressed even when focusing on a very distressing part of the memory (usually because of being under-engaged in
the trauma memory). In these cases, focusing in on the hot spot may
cause increased engagement and a corresponding increase in SUDS before habituation occurs.

When the hot spot work is completed, have the client return to focusing
on and recounting the entire trauma memory, putting it all back together. This should be done in the last session of treatment.

For some clients who experienced multiple traumas or repeated incidents of a particular trauma (e.g., childhood sexual abuse, war), it may
also be necessary to focus the imaginal exposure on several traumatic
memories. We do not move on to another trauma memory until sufficient reduction of anxiety and distress is evident with the first memory.
Because we focus the initial recounting on the "worst" trauma memory,
or the one that seems to be causing the greatest distress or most reexperiencing symptoms at present, the benefits of working through this
memory often generalize to the other trauma memories such that they

are emotionally processed without direct exposure. But if any other memories remain significantly distressing, you may want to devote some sessions to working on these as well.

Processing the Imaginal Exposure (15–20 minutes)

As described in detail in session 3, you will process the imaginal exposure with clients after they have finished revisiting and recounting the trauma. Usually, as treatment progresses and the client gains new perspective and more insight on the trauma, this postexposure discussion takes less time than it did in the early sessions of imaginal exposure. However, sometimes new material emerges in the hot spot work as clients identify the most terrifying moments of the traumatic incidents, e.g., "I thought the next time my parents would see me would be in a coffin," or "I was worried he would hit me in the eyes and blind me and then, even if I survived, I'd never be able to work again." Refer to the description of Processing detailed in session 3 for suggestions on how to conduct the processing.

Discussion of In Vivo Exposure (10–15 minutes)

Proceed with planning daily in vivo exposure homework assignments. You should guide clients in moving up their In Vivo Exposure Hierarchy as treatment progresses. Clients should continue to practice each exposure item until it ceases to produce more than mild anxiety or discomfort. As their symptoms decrease and confidence increases, encourage clients to do as much as they can in order to "take back" their lives and to find ways to do in vivo exposure in day-to-day life.

Homework (5 minutes)

✎ Instruct client to continue breathing practice.

✎ Ask client to listen to imaginal exposure tape daily.

✎ Ask client to continue to practice in vivo exposure exercises.

✎ Client should also listen to the session audiotape one time.

Chapter 7 | *Final Session*

(Corresponds to chapter 8 of the workbook)

Materials Needed

- Audiotape to record entire session

- In Vivo Exposure Hierarchy from session 2

Session Outline

- Review homework (10 minutes)

- Present agenda for session (3 minutes)

- Conduct imaginal exposure (20–30 minutes)

- Review progress and make suggestions for continued practice (30 minutes)

- Terminate therapy: saying goodbye (5 minutes)

Homework Review (10 minutes)

Begin the final session by reviewing the client's homework. Discuss her SUDS ratings of the imaginal and in vivo exposure homework. Inquire about the client's reactions to listening to the imaginal exposure and session tapes. Ask her what she learned this week during her exposure experiences, and offer her much praise and acknowledgment for her hard work.

Set Agenda (3 minutes)

Present the client with the agenda for the session by telling her that you are first going to ask her to revisit and recount her trauma memory, and then you are going to discuss the progress she has made, as well as design a plan for continued work after therapy.

Imaginal Exposure (20–30 minutes)

In this session the client engages in recounting the trauma memory for 20–30 minutes. Ask the client to focus on the entire trauma memory in this revisiting, rather than working on hot spots. It is important to end PE with the client narrating the entire newly organized memory. When the client finishes the exposure, begin the processing by offering praise or positive feedback as usual, but follow this with questions designed to prompt the client to think about how the imaginal exposure has changed for her over the course of therapy. For example: "Great job! You were really pretty calm during the revisiting of your memory today. I'm wondering how this felt to you today, compared with how you felt after doing it that very first time. What is different for you now?" This discussion will lead into an important part of this final session: reviewing what the client has learned in the course of PE, what has changed or improved, and what she needs to continue to do.

Review Treatment Program and Client's Progress (30 minutes)

Information for Therapist

This part of the final session involves an evaluation and discussion of the client's progress. You will also review the skills that she has learned and make recommendations for further treatment if indicated. You will give the client positive feedback for all that she has accomplished in the program and, if terminating treatment now, say goodbye.

This conversation should be interactive and solicit the client's perceptions of her progress, what she has learned, and her sense of readiness to continue the work begun in her therapy. You should ask questions aimed at evaluating her preparedness for using the exposure skills in her daily life. You will also prepare her for the likelihood of an increase in symptoms when under duress or in times of significant stress. The two main objectives in this discussion are: (1) to ensure that the client feels that she can manage temporary increases in PTSD symptoms or stressful events with the coping skills acquired in the treatment program, and (2) to ensure that the client realizes that even though she is doing quite well now, it is likely that due to normal life events she may experience an increase in anxiety, stress, or PTSD-related symptoms. These times should be seen not as relapses, but rather as opportunities to practice the skills she has acquired.

Review of Skills Learned in Program

We have been working together on your PTSD symptoms for about [X] weeks. Today I'd like to review your progress in the program and discuss the skills that you have learned. I'd also like to take a few minutes to say goodbye. We have spent these weeks working together to help you process what happened to you during the trauma by repeatedly recounting it in detail. You have spent quite a lot of time doing in vivo exposure exercises to help you approach people and situations that you've been avoiding. I'd like to talk with you about how you are feeling now, what you found helpful or not helpful during treatment, what additional skills you need to learn, and your plans for the near future.

Review the Client's Progress in In Vivo Exposure

To begin, take out the In Vivo Exposure Hierarchy created in session 2. Without showing it to the client, read each of the situations on the list and ask the client to imagine herself doing each of the things on the hierarchy *right now.* Ask her to give her anticipated SUDS levels for each situation if she were to engage in that situation now. Record these ratings in the last column labeled "Final Session." When completed, show the client the sheet with the two columns of ratings, the first one from session 2 and the one from today. For nearly all clients, there will be significant decreases in SUDS levels for most items on the list. Ask the client, "What do you think of the two sets of ratings? How did you accomplish this remarkable change? What did you do that caused these ratings to go down?"

Note improvement in those situations that changed significantly. Discuss the situations for which the client's SUDS ratings did not decrease as much. Ask, "What do you think happened with this situation? Why has it remained relatively high?" Usually, these are the situations that the client has not confronted sufficiently. Discuss the items on the list that still have high ratings and warrant further exposure work. Help her make a schedule to practice these situations over the next few weeks. Encourage her to face the feared situations and memories as they come up. Have the client record the second set of SUDS ratings on the In Vivo Exposure Hierarchy in her workbook, and note which situations she plans to continue practicing.

After this in-depth discussion of in vivo exposure, review what the client has learned over the course of therapy by asking a variety of additional questions. It is helpful to begin this by talking about how her self-reported PTSD and depression scores have changed from pretreatment levels to now, using the self-report measures of the PDS and the BDI. The aim of this discussion is to help the client articulate what she has learned during PE, and what caused her symptoms to decline and her satisfaction in life to increase. For example:

- So how did you accomplish all of these changes? What did you do in this therapy that brought about this difference?

- What have you noticed about your level of anxiety or discomfort in certain situations?

- What have you learned?

- What have you found most helpful to manage that anxiety and discomfort?

- Are there any problems that you are still concerned about? What do you think you need to do about these?

If warranted by the client's condition, discuss options for referral for further treatment. However, unless immediate therapy is necessary, encourage her to try to use the skills learned in therapy over the next several months and to call you if she runs into difficulties.

- I think you have made some real progress in the program. How are you feeling about these changes?

- How are you feeling now compared with when you began the program?

- What were the most helpful things that we did?

- Was there anything that you didn't find very helpful?

- Are there any skills that you think you need to continue to practice?

- If so, help the client make plans for how she can achieve her goals.

Finally, prepare the client for the likelihood of a temporary increase in PTSD and related symptoms when under significant stress, such as the anniversary of the trauma or more general difficulties at work or in the family. For example, "It's pretty common for people who have recovered from PTSD as you have to find that in periods of great stress in life, even positive life stress (e.g., getting married, having a baby, getting a new job), symptoms can creep up again. It's important to then put this in perspective and to begin using the tools you've learned in this program. What will you do if 2 months from now you suddenly start experiencing intrusive thoughts and nightmares about the trauma again?" or "What will you do if you find yourself in a situation that reminds you strongly of your trauma and it causes you begin feeling afraid of going out again?" or "What will you do when you go through a stressful period of life and you find yourself feeling scared and inadequate?"

If the client has been in therapy with you for other issues, explore with her other areas that need attention. You and the client may choose to continue to work together on other issues.

Termination: Saying Goodbye (5 minutes)

Working with a client in PE can be emotionally intense for both the client and you, so, not surprisingly, terminating therapy can be difficult for the client. Take ample time to do this. Indeed, for many clients, it can be useful to remind them throughout therapy of the relatively short-term nature of the work you are doing together. It may be that you will continue seeing the client for some period of time to work on other problems or issues. But if you are terminating treatment at this point, take time to offer the client feedback and to say goodbye. For example:

- You did a great job with this challenging treatment. I have enjoyed working with you.

- You had some difficult weeks there, but you persisted with courage and patience, and it is obvious that your efforts have paid off for you.

- You mentioned that you were disappointed that you had not made more progress in the program. I'd like to tell you that it is not un-usual for clients to express the same feelings and then discover that they feel much better as time goes on.

- It takes time to digest and process what happened to you in treatment. You may continue to feel better as time goes on, especially if you continue to use the skills and techniques that you have learned.

- I know this program was difficult for you to complete. In fact, there were a few days (weeks) when you wanted to just drop out of treatment. But you had the courage to stick with the program and have made some important progress.

Conclusion

Working with PTSD clients is extremely rewarding for therapists. The availability of effective treatments for PTSD, including PE, allows mental health professionals to positively impact the disrupted lives of chronic PTSD sufferers in a short period of time. However, PTSD symptoms themselves and related comorbidity may hinder the ability of some clients to engage in and benefit from the therapy. It is not uncommon for PTSD sufferers to fail to attend therapy regularly, to drop out prematurely, or to take long, unofficial breaks from treatment. Some clients struggle with avoidance and are reluctant to do exposure homework. Other clients may have difficulty tolerating anxiety or engaging in the trauma memory. Flexibility in the use of PE procedures guided by the treatment rationale and by the manual is often a necessity. We address this in more depth in chapter 8.

The experience of sharing the pain and horror of the trauma memory with a compassionate, understanding, nonjudgmental person is a powerful healing experience that may by itself begin to reduce the client's fear, shame, and PTSD symptoms. Although PE will be challenging at times for the client and the therapist, it is immensely rewarding for both as well. Many clients tell us at the final session that they feel so much better, and many come back after therapy, telling us that they feel like the people they were before the trauma and that they hadn't thought that would be possible. We have heard horrible trauma stories and wondered initially how anyone could get over such an experience, and then they do. PE has allowed us to witness the resilience of the human spirit.

Chapter 8

Anticipating Problems and Tailoring Treatment to the Individual: Promoting Effective Engagement

(Corresponds to chapter 6 of the workbook)

Even with a foundation of strong therapeutic alliance and a clear rationale for treatment that the client understands and accepts, and even when you have followed the procedures described in these chapters, sometimes the client does not seem to improve as much as we would expect. Common obstacles to the expected decreases in PTSD symptoms and related distress include avoidance, being under- or over-engaged during revisiting and recounting the trauma memory, intolerance of emotional distress, and *persistent* dominance of other negative emotions, such as anger. This is where you, the therapist, need to help the client overcome the obstacles. This may mean helping the client to overcome avoidance, modifying procedures in order to either increase or decrease emotional engagement during the revisiting and recounting of the trauma memory, bolstering the client's distress tolerance skills, or helping the client to process other common trauma-related feelings such as anger, shame, sadness, grief, and guilt.

Importance of the Treatment Model

Emotional Processing Theory was described in the introductory chapter of this therapist guide. When trying to decide how to proceed in treatment or when faced with making choices about whether and how to modify PE procedures, a firm grounding in this conceptual model will steer your decision-making process. As discussed in chapter 1, Foa and Kozak (1986) suggested that treatment of pathological fear requires (1) accessing the fear structure (i.e., bringing the person into contact with the feared situation such that their fear structure is activated), and (2) providing corrective information that is a "safe experience" that serves to modify the excessive or unrealistic aspects of the fear structure. The PE therapist should keep in mind these objectives when designing treatment interventions.

For example, a good in vivo exposure hierarchy is composed of exposure situations that match the individual's specific fear structure. For an assault survivor who is excessively fearful of unfamiliar men because "you never know who will hurt you," in vivo assignments might include (1) gradual exposure to interactions with men in safe situations (e.g., asking a male clerk for information in the store, checking out in the grocery store with male cashiers, saying hello and making eye contact with these men, initiating conversations with male coworkers or customers), and (2) remaining unharmed during these experiences (i.e., not being hurt or threatened by these men), thus modifying the client's perception that all men are dangerous.

Theoretical considerations also provide guidance when the need arises to modify treatment. For example, a client who always gives a very cursory account of her trauma in recounting the trauma memory during imaginal exposures and who works hard to keep her feelings shut down while doing so is most likely not accessing her fear structure—she is avoiding the feelings, thoughts, or images that are associated with her trauma memory. You will need to help this client realize that this avoidance, although understandable, interferes with her recovery from PTSD, and work with her to find ways to increase her ability to engage in all of the salient aspects of the trauma memory so that it may be processed.

Understanding the conceptual model underlying PE is an essential starting place. It will help you provide a convincing rationale that makes sense to the client and will bolster her courage and willingness to confront trauma-related situations or memories rather than avoid them. The conceptual model will also guide you in your response to the client's struggles with avoidance behavior. In particular, it will guide your construction of the in vivo hierarchy and help you figure out when and how to modify the standard procedures for imaginal exposure.

Modifying In Vivo Exposure

In session 2, you and the client generated a list of situations, places, people, or activities that the client fears and avoids (or endures if necessary, but as briefly as possible) in an effort not to trigger trauma-related fear or discomfort. You may have also included situations on the initial in vivo hierarchy that were designed to increase the client's opportunities for social interaction or positive experiences or that were aimed at "behavioral activation"—just getting the client busy and engaged in life activities. These situations were ranked according to how much fear or distress they elicited or according to how difficult they seemed to the client. Typically, clients systematically move up the hierarchy, practicing each in vivo exposure repeatedly until the anxiety or distress it arouses is minimal and the person no longer regards the situation as dangerous or difficult to confront.

PTSD clients usually struggle with their tendency to avoid feared situations during treatment. Most clients benefit from ample support and encouragement from you to hang in there and keep working on their in vivo assignments. The urges to avoid are common and understandable, but, as you have explained to the client, avoidance maintains the trauma-related fear and anxiety. When a client has difficulty completing her in vivo exposure assignments, it is often useful to modify the hierarchy by breaking the target situation(s) into smaller, incremental steps. If it becomes evident that an in vivo exposure situation is too difficult to confront at the present time, find ways to make it less difficult or to reduce the client's SUDS level. Sometimes having a friend or family member, or yourself, accompany the client during the exposure exercise helps the client manage the distress associated with that situation and confront the situation alone in subsequent exposure exercises. Changing other factors like time of day or location of the exposure may also decrease the distress associated with the exercise to a manageable degree. When the client has mastered the modified (and relatively easier) exposure situation, she can move on to the one that she could not confront originally and then move on to more difficult situations.

Occasionally, as treatment progresses, a client may not experience the expected fear reduction despite what appears to be systematic and repeated exposure. In these cases, it is helpful to look closely at what the client is actually *doing* during the in vivo exposure exercises. Ask the client exactly how she is carrying out the exposure, how long it lasts, and when she ends it. Is the exposure of sufficient duration? Or is the client escaping the situation while still highly anxious? Also look for subtle avoidance and "safety behaviors" such as being with only "safe" people, shopping only when the stores are not crowded, and always choosing a female clerk or cashier to deal with. These behaviors interfere with fear reduction by maintaining the client's perception that she was not harmed only because of the protective measures she took. This perception, in turn, prevents the client from realizing that the situations are actually not dangerous and do not require protective measures. If you identify such safety behaviors, explain to the client how these subtle avoidance behaviors maintain fear and trauma-related, unrealistic beliefs.

Finally, look for avoidance that the client may not be aware of. One client puzzled us because, although consistently doing her exposure homework between sessions, she was not habituating at all, and at midtreatment her PTSD symptoms were higher than they were at pretreatment. The therapist tried to understand why this lack of progress was occurring by very closely examining the client's behavior. This careful examination revealed that the client was keeping herself emotionally detached while doing her homework; moreover, whenever she was not explicitly doing exposure homework, she was completely and deliberately avoiding all trauma-related cues, thoughts, and feelings. She was not even aware of her extensive avoidance; she did not think of it in terms of avoidance, because she was merely living as she had since her trauma. This lack of generalization or failure to apply what she was learning in treatment to daily life accounted for the persistence of her PTSD and depression symptoms. The therapist helped the client see how her avoidance was interfering with getting benefit from all her hard work, and the client began to recognize and reduce her extensive avoidance behavior in daily life. In turn, her PTSD symptoms quickly began to improve.

Another client reported doing her exposures as instructed, such as spending more time out and alone at night, without apparent benefit.

When details were elicited, it turned out she was preparing her house keys in her hand before she left her car and racing to the front door, and could almost not get the door unlocked fast enough. When she quickly slammed the door, she felt as if she had narrowly escaped danger. The therapist had to explain how conducting exposure in this manner was not *therapeutic*. It was important to let her mind and body learn that she had nothing to fear from the dark outside her front door even if *she took her time and looked for the door keys while standing in front of her door.*

Modifying Imaginal Exposure

In PE, imaginal exposure to trauma memories is conducted in a manner that promotes emotional engagement with the memory and with the feelings generated by facing it. Through repeated imaginal confrontation with the trauma memory, the images, thoughts, and feelings that are part of the fear structure are organized and integrated. Emotional processing is facilitated when the client is emotionally connected with the memory and with the feelings aroused by this process, but at the same time feels in control and is not overwhelmed with anxiety. Imaginal exposure should be conducted in a manner that allows the client to learn that remembering and recounting the traumatic memories is not dangerous and that anxiety does not last indefinitely.

The importance of emotional engagement during the revisiting and recounting of the trauma memory has empirical support. For example, using self-reported distress levels during imaginal exposure to the memory of a traumatic event as an index of emotional engagement, Jaycox, Foa, and Morral (1998) examined the relationship between changes in women's distress levels during six successive sessions of exposure therapy and treatment outcome. Patients who showed high initial distress levels and gradual habituation across sessions benefited more from treatment than those who showed either high or moderate initial distress and no habituation. Thus, Jaycox et al. concluded that the combination of high engagement and habituation over the course of treatment is associated with successful outcome.

The tendency to suppress feelings while thinking about one's trauma is common among PTSD sufferers. Accordingly, the standard procedures for imaginal exposure are designed to promote emotional engagement by asking the client to keep her eyes closed, vividly imagine and visualize the traumatic scene as if it is happening now, use the present tense, and include in the recounting of the trauma the thoughts, emotions, physical sensations, and behaviors that she experienced during the traumatic event. The therapist prompts for details that are missing (e.g., "What are you feeling now?" or "What are you thinking now?") and monitors the client's distress level throughout the revisiting of the trauma. In our experience, the most frequent problem with emotional engagement is under-engagement. Rarely, a client manifests the opposite pattern, namely, being overwhelmed with emotions during the recounting of the trauma memory and feeling loss of control. We term this experience "over-engagement." When a client is not experiencing effective emotional engagement during exposure, the standard procedures for imaginal exposure should be modified to increase or decrease the client's level of arousal or distress accordingly (see below).

Under-Engagement

As used in PE, the term "under-engagement" refers to difficulty accessing the emotional components of the fear structure or trauma memory. It is most commonly encountered in imaginal exposure but may also occur with in vivo exposure. In the case of imaginal exposure, the client may describe her trauma, even in great detail, yet feel disconnected from it emotionally or not be able to visualize what happened. She may report feeling numb or detached. Distress or anxiety levels during the exposure are typically low when the client is under-engaged. Alternatively, the under-engaged client may report high distress levels, yet her nonverbal behaviors such as facial expression, tone of voice, and bodily gestures do not reflect high distress. Sometimes the language used by the under-engaged client seems stilted or distant, as if she is reading a police report rather than giving a first-person account of a traumatic event. For example, the client may refer to an attacker as "the assailant" or "perpetrator" or use other terminology that seems unlikely to have been in her mind at the time of a trauma.

You can encourage emotional engagement first by ensuring that standard procedures are followed, asking the client to keep her eyes closed and use present tense consistently. These procedures promote access of and emotional connection to the memory. Occasionally probe for details, sensory information, feelings, and thoughts (e.g., "Describe what you see; Describe the room; How does it smell? What are you wearing? What are you feeling? What are you thinking?") with brief questions using present tense (e.g., "What do you see?" rather than "What did you see?"). Always direct these brief questions at what the client is describing or visualizing at the moment so that you do not pull her out of her imagery by redirecting her attention.

While such prompting can promote emotional engagement during the recounting of the trauma, it is also important with under-engaged clients to not ask *too* many prompting questions. Doing so may lead to your being too directive or getting into conversations with the client during imaginal exposure that, in turn, reduce rather than promote her connection with the image and emotional engagement with the memory. Your job is to facilitate the client's access of her emotions during the recounting of the traumatic memory but at the same time not to direct it and thereby interfere with the processing of the memory.

If under-engagement is persistent across sessions, revisit the rationale for exposure with the client. Discuss the reasons that you are asking her to emotionally connect to this painful memory, and explain why emotional engagement will promote her recovery from PTSD. Remind her that memories are not dangerous, even though they feel upsetting, and that recounting and visualizing the memory is not the same as reencountering the trauma. If it seems relevant, ask what the client fears will happen if she lets herself feel the emotions associated with this trauma (e.g., "I'll lose control; I'll fall apart; I'll cry; I'll never stop feeling anxious"). Validate the client's feelings, but help her realize that being distressed is not dangerous. It may help to share with the client the research findings that indicate that emotional engagement facilitates recovery. Metaphors may help; for example, ask the client what we can do to help her get around this wall she has built to protect herself from her emotions.

Finally, clients who may not understand what is being asked of them can greatly benefit from you modeling for them how to be emotionally engaged during recounting of the trauma memory. Tell the client that you are going to role play for her and show her how to do the imaginal reliving. By this point, you will know her trauma narrative well. Close your eyes, speak in the present tense, and describe her trauma experience just as you would like her to do, including all of the relevant details, feelings, and thoughts; convey emotion in your voice, facial expression, and bodily movement.

Over-Engagement

As used in PE, the term "over-engagement" refers to excessive emotional distress elicited by imaginal exposure to the trauma memory. Imaginal confrontation with frightening memories or images is often distressing and can elicit tears and emotional upset, especially in the early stage of PE. Thus, it can be difficult to tell when a client has passed from being emotionally upset to being over-engaged. One way that we identify excessive engagement or distress is by asking ourselves whether the client's experience in this moment is conducive to learning. Is the client able to observe and incorporate what is happening to her during imaginal exposure? Or, during imaginal exposure to trauma memories, is the client's experience as though she is *actually* back in the traumatic event? Is she able to learn from this experience that memories are not dangerous, even if painful, that she is not losing her mind, that she is not losing control, and that anxiety does not last indefinitely? If not, the client is likely over-engaged.

In our experience using PE with hundreds of trauma survivors, we have found that very few clients are over-engaged. The few who are can be divided into two types: "dissociative" and "emotionally overwhelmed." Dissociative over-engaged clients have difficulty maintaining a sense of being grounded and safe in the present moment. Recounting the trauma memory feels to them like actually reencountering the trauma. They may have body memories or flashbacks during imaginal exposure. They may be less responsive to the therapist's questions or directions. Their physical movements during exposure may mirror actual actions that took place during the trauma. Distress or SUDS levels are typically extremely high, and habituation does not occur over successive repetitions of exposure. Sometimes the client may feel or appear detached or dissociated from present experience.

Emotionally overwhelmed over-engaged clients usually sob or cry hard for prolonged periods of time. However, you should not regard crying hard as indicative of over-engagement unless it persists during recounting of the trauma memory for several sessions. As mentioned above, many clients find it very distressing to describe and emotionally engage with traumatic experiences, and many people express a high level of distress during imaginal exposure, especially in the first two or three sessions. But when this intensity of emotional distress persists, it will also often be apparent that the client is not really processing or organizing her trauma. She seems stuck. Indeed, sometimes this type of over-engager is not really talking or describing the trauma but is just sobbing or crying. Her behavior may seem regressive or developmentally immature during the imaginal exposure. If you are unsure whether your client is over-engaged or just highly distressed, remember the questions above: Is the client's experience in this moment conducive to learning? Is she moving through her pain to get to the other side of it, or is she stuck in it? Will the client learn anything useful from repeatedly listening to an audiotape of the imaginal exposure? If not, it is best to modify the procedures so as to decrease engagement in exposure.

In modifying the exposure procedures, the primary goal is to help the client to successfully describe some part of the trauma memory while managing her distress and staying grounded in the present, knowing that she is safe here in your office. Discuss the issue with the client, and have her help you figure out ways to provide support and grounding while she recounts the traumatic experience. Revisit the rationale for imaginal exposure as needed, with emphasis on learning to discriminate the actual trauma from its memory: stress that memories may be painful but *are not* dangerous, while the trauma itself *was* dangerous. Modify procedures to reduce emotional engagement during the recounting of the trauma.

A first step with over-engagers is to reverse or change the procedures that are designed to promote engagement: ask the client to keep her eyes open while describing the exposure scene and to use the past rather than present tense in narrating the trauma memory. Sometimes these two modifications alone reduce engagement sufficiently. It is also helpful to be more involved during the client's recounting of the traumatic memory: use your voice to connect with the client and to communicate empathy. These comments should be brief supportive statements that praise and acknowledge the client's effort and encourage her to remain with the memory (e.g., "I know this is really difficult, you are doing a great job"; "I know this is distressing, but you are safe here, the memory can't hurt you"). It may be helpful to remind the client to keep in mind that she made it through the trauma and that she can keep one foot grounded in your office and the other foot in the revisiting of the traumatic memory.

When an over-engaged client is extremely distressed or overwhelmed by recounting and imagining a traumatic memory, it is sometimes best to begin by just having a conversation about the trauma in past tense and with eyes open. The aim is to increase the client's sense of control and competence by disclosing the details of a trauma while maintaining contact with you and feeling supported by you. If the client seems "stuck" at any point during the recounting of the trauma, which happens especially at points that were particularly distressing or horrible, move the memory forward to foster the realization that this moment is in the past by asking, "And then what happened after that?" For some clients, the recounting of the trauma may remain conversational throughout treatment. But if possible, as the client's ability to engage with the traumatic memory grows and her distress decreases, encourage her to recount the trauma with your support and encouragement while reducing the conversation with you.

An alternative procedure for over-engaged clients is writing the trauma narrative instead of recounting it aloud. This can be done during the session and also as homework between sessions. Ask the client to write down what happened and to include thoughts, feelings, actions, and sensations as well as details about the event (e.g., it was dark outside; I was walking on the sidewalk). As the client succeeds in writing the trauma narrative and begins to show habituation and mastery, move into having her read the narrative aloud, or you read it to her. Or take turns reading the narrative, repeating it multiple times within the session.

The therapist may also ask the client if there are other things that can be done to facilitate her feeling of being supported and grounded in the present. Physical touch may be helpful but should always be discussed prior to imaginal exposure or offered verbally during exposure (e.g., "May I touch your hand?" or "I am going to hand you some tissues"). Some clients do not want to be touched at all, while others may find it helpful. Infrequently, we have had clients who coped with distress during exposure by continuously holding the therapist's hand. While in general we do not encourage clients to use breathing training during in vivo or imaginal exposure because it can become a safety behavior, we sometimes instruct the over-engagers to engage in slow, paced breathing as taught in the first session. When clients are especially agitated or physically restless during the recounting of the trauma memory, we may offer them something to manipulate, such as a stress ball or a towel. One former client found that she was able to maintain engagement and also remain grounded in the present by describing her trauma while walking outside with the therapist.

Other Obstacles to Successful Exposure

Avoidance

Confrontation with feared situations or memories often triggers urges to escape or avoid, so avoidance is the most commonly encountered impediment to effective exposure both in and out of the therapist's office. Some clients experience an increase in their urges to avoid after the introduction of in vivo and imaginal exposure, several sessions into treatment. For these clients, this stage of therapy can be seen as "feeling worse before you feel better," and their symptoms may directly reflect this. With extremely avoidant clients, it can be helpful to predict early on that this pattern may happen and let them know that this pattern is not associated with lesser outcome.

When struggles with avoidance are evident, acknowledge the client's anxiety and urges to avoid, and label them as part of their PTSD. At the same time, remind the client that while avoidance reduces anxiety in the short term, in the long run it maintains fear and prevents the client from learning that the avoided situations (or thoughts, memories, impulses, images) are not harmful or dangerous.

In some cases of repeated avoidance behavior, reiterating the exposure rationale, while important, may not be enough. As noted earlier in the chapter, you and the client may need to take a close look at progress with the in vivo exposure exercises and break them down into a more gradual progression. In addition, metaphors or analogies can be a useful tool in helping the client to overcome avoidance. For example, we sometimes describe this struggle as sitting on a fence between exposure and avoidance. We acknowledge the difficulty of getting off the fence but stress that sitting on it prolongs the fear and slows progress. We sometimes encourage the client to "*invite* the feeling" of anxiety in the service of mastery and recovery, rather than only having it triggered against one's will. One of the primary aims of PE is to help the client learn that while anxiety is uncomfortable, it is not dangerous, and treatment involves learning to tolerate the anxiety induced by confronting rather than avoiding trauma-related feared situations and memories.

Finally, it may be helpful to review the reasons that the client sought treatment in the first place (i.e., the ways in which their PTSD symptoms interfere with life satisfaction) and to review the progress that has already been made. Simply revisiting these important issues, while also validating the client's fear and concerns that exposure can be difficult, may help the client to renew her struggle against avoidance.

Anger and Other Negative Emotions

While exposure therapy was originally conceived as a treatment for the reduction of excessive or pathological anxiety, our experience over years of treating PTSD sufferers has taught us that PE facilitates the emotional processing of much more than fear and anxiety. Strong emotions are often stirred and activated in the process of PE. Clients commonly report feelings of anger, rage, sadness, grief, shame, and guilt during imaginal exposure and at other points in processing their traumas. Of these, anger has perhaps received the most attention thus far.

The experience and expression of intense anger during the recounting of the traumatic memory may interfere with emotional processing by dominating the client's affect and preventing engagement with the core fear associated with the traumatic memory. Some empirical findings have supported this concern (Foa, Riggs, Massie, & Yarczower, 1995). Accordingly, in the treatment of PTSD, when a client primarily expresses anger and rage, we first validate that feeling as an appropriate response to the trauma and as a symptom of PTSD. We then present the idea that focusing on the anger during exposure may prevent the client from engaging with the fear and anxiety associated with the trauma memory and thus impede emotional processing and recovery. If needed, we encourage the client to direct the energy of her anger toward getting better and/or to "move it aside" in order to focus on other equally important elements of her experience. Repeated conversations during the processing phase over the course of treatment may be needed when engagement with the memory and other trauma reminders trigger intense anger.

Notably, using a subset of the participants in the Foa, Dancu, et al. (1999) PTSD treatment outcome study, Cahill, Rauch, Hembree, and Foa (2003) examined changes in self-reported anger over the course of treatment and found that the PE, SIT, and PE/SIT treatments resulted in significant decreases in anger even though treatment was focused on reduction of fear.

We have come to know PE as a powerful vehicle for eliciting and emotionally processing an array of intense emotional responses to trauma and its aftermath. These varied emotions and the thoughts and beliefs they are associated with are discussed in the post-imaginal exposure processing part of the session, as you try to help the client incorporate them in developing a more realistic, accurate perspective on the traumatic event(s).

Chaos and Crises: Maintaining the Focus of Treatment on PTSD

As described in chapter 2, comorbidity of other psychiatric disorders with chronic PTSD is quite high. Depression, dysthymia, other anxiety disorders, and alcohol and substance abuse and dependence are common. In addition, clients with chronic PTSD often face multiple life stressors, leading to chaotic lifestyles. Therefore, crises during treatment are quite usual, especially if early or multiple traumatic experiences have interfered with the development of healthy coping skills. Poorly modulated affect, self-destructive impulse control problems (e.g., alcohol binges, risky behaviors), numerous conflicts with family members or others, and severe depression with suicidal ideation are common with chronic PTSD. These problems require attention but can potentially disrupt the focus on treatment of PTSD. As described in chapter 2 of this therapist guide, if careful pretreatment assessment has determined that chronic PTSD is among the client's primary problems, our approach is to maintain the focus on PTSD with periodic reassessment of other problem areas as needed.

If the client's mood or behavior cause imminent concern about her personal safety or the safety of others, the need to attend to this prominent risk may require postponing PE. However, if a crisis arises without imminent risk, we explain to the client that adhering to the treatment plan, and thereby decreasing PTSD symptoms and associated problems, is the best help we can offer. In maintaining this focus, the therapist must clearly express support for the client's desire to recover from PTSD. Communicate a strong belief that the client wants to get better, and applaud every step in the direction of healthy coping and adherence to the treatment program. If appropriate, the therapist may label and externalize crises as related to the PTSD and predict that these situations will improve as the client's skills improve and PTSD symptoms decline. The aim is to provide emotional support throughout the crisis and at the same time keep PTSD as the major focus of treatment.

In their review of cognitive behavioral interventions for PTSD, Rothbaum et al. (2000) noted that some findings suggest that not everyone may be a candidate for exposure therapy. This may include trauma survivors who are unwilling to confront trauma reminders or memories or to tolerate temporarily increased levels of anxiety and PTSD symptoms, individuals who are perpetrators of harm, especially where guilt is the predominant emotion, and perhaps those whose primary emotional response to trauma is anger (cf. Foa, Molnar, and Cashman, 1995). The findings of Cahill et al. (2003) do not support the exclusion of the latter group from PE, however. Rothbaum et al. (2000) also concluded that even with these limitations, exposure therapy has received the strongest evidence in support of its efficacy in reducing PTSD and should be considered a first-line intervention unless ruled out for some reason. We recommend that even when crises arise, if possible, find a way to keep PE as the focus of your treatment. Reducing PTSD, depression, and related symptoms, as well as increasing the client's sense of confidence and self-efficacy, will facilitate the client's ability to cope better with crises in the future as well as to prevent them.

Appendix A *Trauma Interview (for Therapist's Use in Session 1)*

TRAUMA INTERVIEW

Client: _____   Date: _____

Therapist: _____

Note: This interview is structured on the assumption that a thorough **assessment or intake has already been conducted, that this evaluation confirmed the experience of at least one** *DSM-IV* **Criterion A trauma and the diagnosis of PTSD or significant symptoms of PTSD,** and that the therapist has reviewed this information.

Age: _____   Educational level: _____   Date of birth: _____

Race: _____
    1 - African American   5 - Asian/Pacific Islander
    2 - Biracial   6 - Spanish Origin
    3 - Caucasian   7 - Other
    4 - Native American   8 - Unknown

Marital Status: _____   Living with: _____   Work Status: _____

Current employment or job: _____

Psychiatric diagnoses or conditions (obtain before session from initial evaluation; review as needed):

_____

_____

_____

_____

Any other current treatments (may obtain from initial evaluation or ask as needed):

_____

_____

_____

_____

_____

SAY TO THE CLIENT: I'm going to ask you some questions about the trauma and how you have been feeling and doing lately or since the time of the trauma. Some of what we will discuss may be difficult for you to talk about. If there is anything I can do to make our conversation less difficult for you, please let me know. Do you have any questions before we begin?

I have information from your initial assessment (or intake) with _____ [name intake assessor if not self], so I know what you told him/her about your trauma. I understand from his/her notes that . . . *[**Briefly** summarize the trauma information obtained in the intake.]*

Is that about right? Is there anything you would like to add?

_____

_____

_____

_____

_____

Sometimes people have experienced other traumatic events at other times in their lives. Has this happened in your life? Have you ever experienced, or witnessed, or been confronted with other traumatic events?

_____

_____

_____

_____

_____

Note to clinician: If client is unsure, you may want to list all or some of the following to give him/her an idea of what comprises a Criterion A trauma:

Natural disaster (e.g., tornado, hurricane, fire, or flood)

Serious accident or serious injury

Combat or being in a combat zone

Sudden life-threatening illness

Accidental death or murder of a close friend or family member

Suicide of a close friend or family member

Being attacked with a gun, knife, or other weapon

Attacked without a weapon but with the intent to kill or seriously injure

Severely beaten (i.e., beatings that left marks or bruises), or witnessing severe physical violence

Sexual abuse as a child or adolescent

Physical force or the threat of physical force leading to unwanted sexual contact

Rape or attempted rape

Aggravated assault

IDENTIFICATION OF TARGET TRAUMA (i.e., the one that will be of primary focus in PE treatment)

SAY TO THE CLIENT: Of all these things that happened to you *[summarize traumatic events endorsed by client]*, which one is currently bothering you the most? Which causes you the most distress? *[Use additional probe questions as needed if the client has difficulty identifying an event; e.g., "Which one most often comes into your thoughts when you don't want to think about it? Which one upsets you the most? Which one is the worst? In which event were you most afraid?"]*

Specify target trauma: _____

SAY TO THE CLIENT: Do you remember what you were thinking and feeling at the time? When it was happening, did you think you would be killed or seriously hurt?

No ☐   Yes ☐

During the _____ [insert identified trauma], did you feel helpless, horrified, or terrified?

No ☐   Yes ☐

If there was an assailant or perpetrator(s), who was it/who were they?

1 - Stranger	9 - Boyfriend/girlfriend
2 - Acquaintance	10 - Husband/wife/partner
3 - Enemy	11 - Organization
4 - Terrorist	12 - Authority figure (specify) _____
5 - Friend	13 - Relative
6 - Parent	14 - Neighbor
7 - Sibling	15 - Other _____
8 - Clergy member	16 - Unknown _____

Where did the trauma occur?

1 - Own residence	6 - School	11 - Car, bus, train, plane
2 - Assailant's residence	7 - Institution	12 - Workplace
3 - Friend/relative's residence	8 - Battlefield	13 - Other (describe) _____
4 - Park, street, alley	9 - Public place	_____
5 - Parking lot/garage	10 - Abandoned property	_____

What, if any, physical injuries did you have? Have these injuries continued to cause or to be a problem for you?

_____

_____

_____

_____

Were you given medical attention? Was it helpful? Are you still under medical care for these injuries or problems?

_____

_____

_____

_____

Has any criminal or legal action resulted from this trauma? What is the status of that now? (If appropriate:) How is that affecting you?

_____

_____

_____

_____

SAY TO THE CLIENT: I'm going to ask you some questions now about who, if anyone, you blame for the occurrence of this trauma. I want you to know that there are no right or wrong answers to these questions, and we don't think that it is necessary that you place blame. We ask them because it is often helpful to me in our work together to understand how YOU view this event and how you have responded to it. OK?

Who, if anyone, do you blame for the occurrence of the trauma?

1 - Myself   5 - Friend or acquaintance
2 - Assailant(s) or perpetrators   6 - The environment
3 - An organization   7 - Chance
4 - The government   8 - Other (describe) _____

How so? (i.e., how is the person or organization responsible?)

_____

_____

_____

_____

Have you been feeling guilty about the trauma or your response to it? Shamed? Angry? How much have these feelings been present for you?

_____

_____

_____

_____

Physical and Mental Health Since Trauma

How has your physical health been since the trauma? (Or, if trauma was long ago: how has your health been lately?)

☐ Good   ☐ Fair   ☐ Poor

What health problems, if any, are you having? Are these related to the trauma?

_____

_____

_____

_____

_____

How is your support system? Who do you like to spend time with or talk to? Have you been connecting with your friends and family lately?

_____

_____

_____

_____

How has your mood been since the trauma? (Or, if trauma was long ago: how has your mood been lately?) Have you been feeling down or depressed? Are you as interested in things as you usually are?

_____

_____

_____

_____

Note: Even if client does not endorse depressed mood, ask the following questions about suicidal ideation and behavior:

Since the trauma, have you ever thought that life is not worth living, or thought about suicide? If yes, how often?

_____

_____

_____

_____

Have you gone so far as to make a careful plan as to how you would kill yourself? Have you taken any action on this (e.g., selected a location or date, bought a gun, obtained pills)?

_____

_____

_____

_____

_____

Do you intend to act on this plan or intend to hurt yourself?

_____

_____

_____

_____

Have you made a suicide attempt since the trauma or at any time? When? (Assess as needed.)

_____

_____

_____

_____

Have you ever deliberately hurt yourself in any way? (If necessary: For example, people some-times scratch or cut or burn themselves on purpose, or otherwise act in potentially self-harming ways.) **Ask as needed:** What do you do to harm yourself? When did you last hurt yourself? How do you manage the urges now if you don't act on them?

If yes, describe:

_____

_____

_____

_____

Have you sought psychiatric or psychological help as a result of the trauma? Crisis intervention? (not including this treatment)

      No ☐   Yes ☐

If yes, describe:

_____

_____

_____

_____

_____

Have you been to the hospital since the trauma for an emotional or nervous condition? Suicide attempt? Alcohol or drug treatment?

No ☐   Yes ☐

Tell me why you were hospitalized:

_____

_____

_____

_____

Summarize current risk assessment and plan if indicated:

_____

_____

_____

_____

Alcohol and Drug Use

I'd like to ask you about your use of drugs or medications. Since the trauma, have you used: (Go through each of the categories below)

Prescription medications (Note specific meds and frequency of use) _____

_____

_____

Street drugs (Note types and frequency of use) _____

_____

_____

Over-the-counter medications (Note type and frequency of use) _____

_____

_____

On average, about how many drinks containing alcohol do you have per day? (Consider one drink to be a 12-ounce can of beer, one cocktail, or a 4-ounce glass of wine.) Has your pattern of use changed since the trauma? If yes, how so?

_____

_____

Have you ever had legal, social, or employment problems because of your alcohol or drug use?

       No ☐   Yes ☐

Do you consider yourself to have a drinking or a drug problem?

       No ☐   Yes ☐

Is there anything else about your life now or about how the PTSD is affecting you that you think I should know now?

_____

_____

_____

_____

Appendix B   *In Vivo Exposure Hierarchy*

In Vivo Exposure Hierarchy

Name: _____

Date: _____

Therapist: _____

SUDS Anchor Points

0— _____

50— _____

100— _____

Item	SUDS (Sess. 2)	SUDS (Final Sess.)
1. _____	_____	_____
2. _____	_____	_____
3. _____	_____	_____
4 _____	_____	_____
5. _____	_____	_____
6. _____	_____	_____
7. _____	_____	_____
8. _____	_____	_____
9. _____	_____	_____
10. _____	_____	_____
11. _____	_____	_____
12. _____	_____	_____
13. _____	_____	_____
14. _____	_____	_____
15. _____	_____	_____
16. _____	_____	_____
17. _____	_____	_____
18. _____	_____	_____

References

American Psychiatric Association. (2000). *Diagnostic and statistical manual of mental disorders (4th ed.)—Text Revision.* Washington, DC: Author.

Amir, N., Stafford, J., Freshman, M. S., & Foa, E. B. (1998). Relationship between trauma narratives and trauma pathology. *Journal of Traumatic Stress, 11,* 385–392.

Barlow, D. H. (2004). Psychological treatments. *American Psychologist, 59,* 869–878.

Beck, A. T., Ward, C. H., Mendelson, M., Mock, J., & Erbaugh, J. (1961). An inventory for measuring depression. *Archives of General Psychiatry, 4,* 561–571.

Breslau, N. (1998). Epidemiology of trauma and posttraumatic stress disorder. In R. Yehuda (Ed.), *Psychological trauma* (pp. 1–29). Washington, DC: American Psychiatric Press.

Breslau, N., Davis, G. C., Andreski, P., & Peterson, E. (1991). Traumatic events and posttraumatic stress disorder in an urban population of young adults. *Archives of General Psychiatry, 48,* 216–222.

Cahill, S. P., & Foa, E. B. (2004). A glass half empty or half full? Where we are and directions for future research in the treatment of PTSD. In S. Taylor (Ed.), *Advances in the treatment of posttraumatic stress disorder: Cognitive-behavioral perspectives* (pp. 267–313). New York: Springer.

Cahill, S. P., Hembree, E. A., & Foa, E. B. (2006). Dissemination of prolonged exposure therapy for posttraumatic stress disorder: Successes and challenges. In Y. Neria, R. Gross, R. Marshall, & E. Susser (Eds.), *Mental health in the wake of terrorist attacks* (pp. 475–492). Cambridge: Cambridge University Press.

Cahill, S. P., Rauch, S. A. M., Hembree, E. A., & Foa, E. B. (2003). Effectiveness of cognitive behavioral treatments for PTSD on anger. *Journal of Cognitive Psychotherapy, 17*(2), 113–131.

Feeny, N. C., Zoellner, L. A., & Foa, E. B. (2002). Treatment outcome for chronic PTSD among female assault victims with borderline personality characteristics: A preliminary examination. *Journal of Personality Disorders, 16,* 30–40.

First, M. B., Spitzer, R. L., Gibbon, M., & Williams, J. B. (1995). *Structured Clinical Interview for DSM-IV Axis I Disorders—Patient Edition (SCID-I/P, Version 2).* New York: Biometrics Research Department, New York State Psychiatric Institute.

Foa, E. B., & Cahill, S. P. (2001). Psychological therapies: Emotional processing. In N. J. Smelser & P. B. Bates (Eds.), *International encyclopedia of the social and behavioral sciences* (pp. 12363–12369). Oxford: Elsevier.

Foa, E. B., Cashman, L., Jaycox, L., & Perry, K. (1997). The validation of a self-report measure of posttraumatic stress disorder: The Posttraumatic Diagnostic Scale. *Psychological Assessment, 9,* 445–451.

Foa, E. B., Dancu, C. V., Hembree, E. A., Jaycox, L. H., Meadows, E. A., & Street, G. P. (1999). A comparison of exposure therapy, stress inoculation training, and their combination for reducing posttraumatic stress disorder in female assault victims. *Journal of Consulting and Clinical Psychology, 67,* 194–200.

Foa, E. B., Davidson, J. R. T., & Frances, A. (1999). The expert consensus guideline series: Treatment of posttraumatic stress disorder. *Journal of Clinical Psychiatry, 60,* 4–76.

Foa, E. B., Hembree, E. A., Cahill, S. P., Rauch, S. A., Riggs, D. S., Feeny, N. C., and Yadin, E. (2005). Randomized trial of prolonged exposure for PTSD with and without cognitive restructuring: Outcome at academic and community clinics. *Journal of Consulting and Clinical Psychology, 73,* 953–964.

Foa, E. B., Huppert, J. D., & Cahill, S. P. (2006). Emotional processing theory: An update. In B. O. Rothbaum (Ed.), *The nature and treatment of pathological anxiety* (pp. 3–24). New York: Guilford Press.

Foa, E. B., & Jaycox, L. H. (1999). Cognitive-behavioral theory and treatment of posttraumatic stress disorder. In D. Spiegel (Ed.), *Efficacy and cost-effectiveness of psychotherapy* (pp. 23–61). Washington, DC: American Psychiatric Press.

Foa, E. B., & Kozak, M. J. (1985). Treatment of anxiety disorders: Implications for psychopathology. In A. H. Tuma & J. D. Maser (Eds.), *Anxiety and the anxiety disorders* (pp. 421–452). Hillsdale, NJ: Erlbaum.

Foa, E. B., & Kozak, M. J. (1986). Emotional processing of fear: Exposure to corrective information. *Psychological Bulletin, 99,* 20–35.

Foa, E. B., & Meadows, E. A. (1997). Psychosocial treatments for posttraumatic stress disorder: A critical review. In J. Spence, J. M. Darley,

& D. J. Foss (Eds.), *Annual Review of Psychology, Vol. 48* (pp. 449–480). Palo Alto, CA: Annual Reviews.

Foa, E. B., Molnar, C., & Cashman, L. (1995). Change in rape narratives during exposure therapy for posttraumatic stress disorder. *Journal of Traumatic Stress—Special Research on Traumatic Memory, 8, 675–690.*

Foa, E. B., & Riggs, D. S. (1993). Post-traumatic stress disorder in rape victims. In J. Oldham, M. B. Riba, & A. Tasman (Eds.), *American Psychiatric Press Review of Psychiatry, Vol. 12* (pp. 285–309). Washington, DC: American Psychiatric Press.

Foa, E. B., Riggs, D. S., Massie, E. D., & Yarczower, M. (1995). The impact of fear activation and anger on the efficacy of exposure treatment for posttraumatic stress disorder. *Behavior Therapy, 26, 487–499.*

Foa, E. B., & Rothbaum, B. O. (1998). *Treating the trauma of rape: Cognitive-behavioral therapy for PTSD.* New York: Guilford Press.

Foa, E. B., Rothbaum, B. O., & Furr, J. M. (2003). Augmenting exposure therapy with other CBT procedures. *Psychiatric Annals, 33, 47–53.*

Foa, E. B., Rothbaum, R. O., Riggs, D. S., & Murdock, T. B. (1991). Treatment of posttraumatic stress disorder in rape victims: A comparison between cognitive-behavioral procedures and counseling. *Journal of Consulting and Clinical Psychology, 59, 715–723.*

Foa, E. B., Steketee, G. S., & Rothbaum, B. O. (1989). Behavioral/cognitive conceptualizations of post-traumatic stress disorder. *Behavior Therapy, 20, 155–176.*

Foa, E. B., Zoellner, L. A., Feeny, N. C., Hembree, E. A., & Alvarez-Conrad, J. (2002). Does imaginal exposure exacerbate PTSD symptoms? *Journal of Consulting and Clinical Psychology, 70, 1022–1028.*

Friedman, M. J., Davidson, J. R. T., Mellman, T. A., & Southwick, S. M. (2000). Pharmacotherapy. In E. Foa, T. Keane, & M. Friedman (Eds.), *Effective treatments for PTSD: Practice guidelines from the International Society for Traumatic Stress Studies* (pp. 84–105). New York: Guilford.

Harvey, A. G., Bryant, R. A., & Tarrier, N. (2003). Cognitive behaviour therapy for posttraumatic stress disorder. *Clinical Psychology Review, 23, 501–522.*

Hembree, E. A., Foa, E. B., Dorfan, N. M., Street, G., Kowalski, J., & Tu, X. (2003). Do patients drop out prematurely from exposure therapy for PTSD? *Journal of Traumatic Stress, 16*(6), 555–562.

Hembree, E. A., Rauch, S. A. M., & Foa, E. B. (2003). Beyond the manual: The insider's guide to prolonged exposure therapy for PTSD. *Cognitive and Behavioral Practice, 10, 22–30.*

Institute of Medicine. (2001). *Crossing the quality chasm: A new health system for the 21st century*. Washington, DC: National Academy Press.

Jaycox, L. H., Foa, E. B., & Morral, A. R. (1998). Influence of emotional engagement and habituation on exposure therapy for PTSD. *Journal of Consulting and Clinical Psychology, 66*, 185–192.

Kessler, R. C., Sonnega, A., Bromet, E., Hughes, M., & Nelson, C. B. (1995). Posttraumatic stress disorder in the National Comorbidity Survey. *Archives of General Psychiatry, 52*, 1048–1060.

Kilpatrick, D. G., Resnick, H. S., & Freedy, J. R. (May 1992). *Post-traumatic stress disorder field trial report: A comprehensive review of the initial results*. Paper presented at the annual meeting of the American Psychiatric Association. Washington, DC.

Nacasch, N., Cohen-Rapperot, G., Polliack, M., Knobler, H. Y., Zohar, J., & Foa, E. B. (2003, April). Prolonged exposure therapy for PTSD: The dissemination and the preliminary results of the implementation of the treatment protocol in Israel [Abstract]. *Proceedings of the 11th Conference of the Israel Psychiatric Association, Haifa, Israel.*

Resick, P. A., Pallavi, N., Weaver, T. L., Astin, M. C., & Feuer, C. A. (2002). A comparison of cognitive-processing therapy with prolonged exposure and a waiting condition for the treatment of chronic posttraumatic stress disorder in female rape victims. *Journal of Consulting and Clinical Psychology, 70*, 867–879.

Riggs, D. S., Rothbaum, B. O., & Foa, E. B. (1995). A prospective examination of symptoms of posttraumatic stress disorder in victims of nonsexual assault. *Journal of Interpersonal Violence, 10*, 201–214.

Rogers, P., Gray, N. S., Williams, T., & Kitchiner, N. (2000). Behavioral treatment of PTSD in a perpetrator of manslaughter: A single case study. *Journal of Traumatic Stress, 13*, 511–519.

Rothbaum, B. O., Astin, M. C., & Marsteller, F. (2005). Prolonged exposure versus eye movement desensitization and reprocessing (EMDR) for PTSD rape victims. *Journal of Traumatic Stress, 18*, 607–616.

Rothbaum, B. O., Cahill, S. P., Foa, E. B., Davidson, J. R. T., Compton, J., Connor, K., Astin, M., & Hahn, C.-G. (2006). Augmentation of sertraline with prolonged exposure in the treatment of PTSD. *Journal of Traumatic Stress, 19*, 625–638.

Rothbaum, B. O., Foa, E. B., Riggs, D. S., Murdock, T., & Walsh, W. (1992). A prospective examination of post-traumatic stress disorder in rape victims. *Journal of Traumatic Stress, 5*, 455–475.

Rothbaum, B. O., Meadows, E. A., Resick, P., & Foy, D. W. (2000). Cognitive-behavioral therapy. In E. B. Foa, T. M. Keane, & M. J. Friedman

(Eds.), *Effective treatments for PTSD: Practice guidelines from the International Society for Traumatic Stress Studies* (pp. 60–83). New York: Guilford Press.

Rothbaum, B. O., Ruef, A. M., Litz, B. T., Han, H., & Hodges, L. (2003). Virtual reality exposure therapy of combat-related PTSD: A case study using psychophysiological indicators of outcome. *Journal of Cognitive Psychotherapy: An International Quarterly, 17,* 163–178.

Schnurr, P. P., & Green, B. L. (2004). Understanding relationships among trauma, post-traumatic stress disorder, and health outcomes. *Advances in Mind-Body Medicine, 20,* 18–29.

Shapiro, F. (1989). Eye movement desensitization: A new treatment for post-traumatic stress disorder. *Journal of Behavior Therapy and Experimental Psychiatry, 20,* 211–217.

Shapiro, F. (1995). *Eye movement desensitization and reprocessing: Basic principles, protocols, and procedures.* New York: Guilford Press.

Tolin, D. F., & Foa, E. B. (2006). Sex differences in trauma and posttraumatic stress disorder: A quantitative review of 25 years of research. *Psychological Bulletin, 132,* 959–992.

About the Authors

Edna B. Foa, PhD, is a professor of clinical psychology in psychiatry at the University of Pennsylvania and director of the Center for the Treatment and Study of Anxiety. She received her PhD in clinical psychology and personality from the University of Missouri, Columbia, in 1970. Dr. Foa has devoted her academic career to studying the psychopathology and treatment of anxiety disorders, primarily obsessive-compulsive disorder (OCD), posttraumatic stress disorder (PTSD), and social phobia, and is currently one of the world's leading experts in these areas. Dr. Foa was the chair of the DSM-IV Subcommittee for OCD and cochaired the DSM-IV Subcommittee for PTSD. She has also been the chair for the Treatment Guidelines Task Force of the International Society for Traumatic Stress Studies.

Dr. Foa has published several books and over 250 articles and book chapters and has lectured extensively around the world. Her work has been recognized with numerous awards and honors. Among them are the Distinguished Professor Award under the Fulbright Program for International Exchange of Scholars; the Distinguished Scientist Award from the American Psychological Association, Society for a Science of Clinical Psychology; the First Annual Outstanding Research Contribution Award presented by the Association for the Advancement of Behavior Therapy; the Distinguished Scientific Contributions to Clinical Psychology Award from the American Psychological Association; the Lifetime Achievement Award presented by the International Society for Traumatic Stress Studies; and the 2006 Senior Scholar Fulbright Award.

Elizabeth A. Hembree, PhD, is an assistant professor of psychology in psychiatry at the University of Pennsylvania School of Medicine. She is the director of training and the director of the Rape and Crime Victims

Program in the Center for the Treatment and Study of Anxiety. Dr. Hembree received her PhD in clinical psychology from the University of Delaware in 1990. Her primary interest and research focus is the investigation and dissemination of cognitive behavioral treatment for PTSD. Dr. Hembree's scholarly publications include scientific articles and book chapters on the treatment of PTSD and OCD. She has been invited to speak internationally and has taught numerous workshops on the use of Prolonged Exposure Therapy (PE) for the treatment of PTSD.

Barbara Olasov Rothbaum, PhD, is a professor in psychiatry at the Emory University School of Medicine in the Department of Psychiatry and Behavioral Sciences and director of the Trauma and Anxiety Recovery Program at Emory. Dr. Rothbaum specializes in research on the treatment of individuals with affective disorders, particularly focusing on anxiety and PTSD. She has won both state and national awards for her research, is an invited speaker internationally, authors scientific papers and chapters, has published and edited several books on the treatment of PTSD, and received the Diplomate in Behavioral Psychology from the American Board of Professional Psychology. She is the immediate past president of the International Society of Traumatic Stress Studies (ISTSS). Dr. Rothbaum is also a pioneer in the application of virtual reality to the treatment of psychological disorders.